Family Circle Holiday & Special Occasions Cookbook

Introduction

Through the centuries, special days or events have been celebrated. At one time, most of these occasions had a religious significance and were known as "holy days." From this term is derived the singular word "holiday."

Whenever you begin to plan a holiday celebration, quite automatically you turn to food. Here is a collection of menus and recipes to help you celebrate holidays and special occasions throughout the year. The recipes have appeared in previous issues of *Family Circle,* the world's leading women's service magazine. The recipes, compiled by food expert Lucy Wing, were created by the magazine's distinguished food department. Each has been triple-tested to reflect today's tastes and utilize the latest equipment and techniques.

The first section features menus and recipes for religious holidays such as Easter, Passover, Hanukkah and Christmas. There are also menus for patriotic celebrations such as Memorial Day, Independence Day and Labor Day. Our Mother's Day Menu is simple enough for children to prepare, while Thanksgiving features an elaborate spread.

In the second section, you'll find menus and recipes for special occasions such as a child's birthday, an anniversary or a wedding. There is an assortment of cookie recipes and a collection of cakes for any special occasion. You'll also find recipes for gourmet foods to make and give.

Whether you are a novice or a seasoned cook, this book will increase your repertoire.

Family Circle Staff

Project Editor	Lucy Wing
Food Editor	Jean Hewitt
Senior Associate Food Editor	Jane O'Keefe
Art Director	Joseph Taveroni
Copy Editor	Susan Tierney
General Manager	John Jaxheimer
Project Manager	Annabelle Arenz

Ideals Publishing Staff

Project Editor	Julie Hogan
Food Stylist	Susan Noland
Photographer	Gerald Koser
Project Management	James Kuse
	Marybeth Owens

COVER: Christmas Buffet Menu: Three Vegetable Pâté, page 89; Regal Crown Roast of Pork with Sweet and Sour Red Cabbage in Apples, page 91; Creamy Baked Onions and Green Beans, page 91

Contents

Photographs by: Richard Jeffery, Allen H. Lieberman, Bill McGinn, Rudy Muller, George Nordhausen, Gordon E. Smith, Rene Velez

ISBN 0-8249-9100-1

Published by Ideals Publishing Corporation
11315 Watertown Plank Road
Milwaukee, WI 53226

RING IN THE NEW YEAR

MAKE A RESOLUTION TO SERVE FABULOUS FOODS.

Herald the New Year with an elegant New Year's Eve Supper, a marvelous late-morning brunch and a bowl game buffet. Here are some menus that should be music to your ears. All the foods can be prepared ahead so that they are ready and waiting for you and your guests. It lets you serve the most fabulous foods in great style and with very little effort. There's little to no strain to spoil your fun. These luscious dishes can be made days ahead and reheated, or simply set out minutes before party time. The New Year's Eve menu offers two quiches—one made with smoked salmon and the other with zucchini and sausage—which are served with an avocado, orange and lettuce salad. To top off this light, late-evening meal, in place of a dessert, let your guests personalize their coffee with some special additions. Serve a pot of dark, fragrant espresso with a selection of liqueurs and brandy. Have a bowl of softly whipped cream and a shaker of cinnamon for those who may want to make cappuccino. At midnight, uncork the champagne and serve with frosted grapes and cookies along with the noisemakers and hats. Making noise to welcome the New Year is an old custom to drive away evil spirits. A late-morning brunch is a great way to begin the first day of the New Year and it's ideal for a casual get-together with friends. For years, the classic New Year's Day parades and bowl games have hypnotized people in front of their television screens. Often dinner is sidelined in favor of the game. It's now chic to serve dinner on a tray in front of the set. Kick off the meal with tasty finger foods. You're sure to score with the glazed beef brisket. So, usher in the New Year with our menus.

NEW YEAR'S EVE SUPPER

Vegetable Crudités Bouquet
(An arrangement of cut-up raw vegetables such as cauliflowerets, carrot slices, radish roses, green and red pepper strips, cucumber sticks and green onions around a bowl of dip.)
Garden Onion Dip*
Mixed Nuts with Raisins
Smoked Salmon Quiche*
Zucchini and Italian Sausage Quiche*
Avocado, Orange and Lettuce Salad
Italian Dressing
Assorted Liqueurs   Whipped Cream
Demitasse Coffee
Sugar-Frosted Green and Red Grapes*
Almond Macaroons*
Champagne

*Recipe given

GARDEN ONION DIP

A refreshing way to vary the all-time favorite party dip. Serve with cucumber and carrot sticks or other vegetables.
Makes 2 cups.

- **1 container (16 ounces) dairy sour cream**
- **1 envelope dehydrated onion soup mix**
- **¼ cup finely diced radish**
- **¼ cup finely diced carrot**
- **¼ cup finely diced green pepper**
- **¼ cup finely diced celery**

1. Combine sour cream, onion soup mix and diced vegetables in a medium-size bowl and blend well. Cover and refrigerate 1 hour or longer.
2. Stir dip just before serving and spoon into serving bowl.

SMOKED SALMON QUICHE

Make-ahead Notes: Prebake pastry shell. Chop salmon and shred cheese. Refrigerate all three. One hour before serving, heat oven and fill shell, following recipe from Step 3. Or, bake quiche early in day and refrigerate. Reheat in moderate oven (350°) for 30 minutes. Prebake shell at 450° for 8 minutes; bake quiche at 450° for 15 minutes, then at 350° for 15 minutes.
Makes 8 servings.

- **1 package piecrust mix**
- **½ pound smoked salmon, chopped**
- **4 ounces Swiss cheese, shredded (1 cup)**
- **4 eggs**
- **1 cup milk**
- **½ cup heavy cream**
- **¼ cup grated Parmesan cheese**
- **1 tablespoon finely chopped fresh dill**
  OR: **1 teaspoon dillweed**
- **½ teaspoon salt**
- **¼ teaspoon pepper**
  Red caviar

1. Preheat oven to 450°. Prepare piecrust mix following label directions. Roll out to a 14-inch round on a lightly floured surface; fit into a 10-inch (6-cup) fluted quiche dish (or use a 10-inch pie plate). Trim pastry overhang to ½ inch and turn under; flute to make a stand-up edge. Prick shell well over entire surface with a fork.
2. Bake in a preheated hot oven (450°) for 8 minutes; remove to wire rack; cool slightly.
3. Spread salmon evenly over bottom of pastry shell; sprinkle Swiss cheese over salmon.
4. Beat eggs lightly in a medium-size bowl. Add milk, heavy cream, Parmesan cheese, dill, salt and pepper; blend well. Pour into pastry shell.
5. Bake in a preheated hot oven (450°) for 15 minutes; lower oven temperature to moderate (350°) and bake 15 minutes or until center is almost firm but still soft. Let stand 15 minutes before serving. Garnish with red caviar and fresh dill, if you wish.

New Year's Eve Supper: Smoked Salmon Quiche, page 5; Zucchini and Italian Sausage Quiche, page 6

ZUCCHINI AND ITALIAN SAUSAGE QUICHE

Make-ahead Note: Prebake pastry shell. Cook zucchini and sausage; prepare milk-egg mixture. Shred cheese. Refrigerate all. One hour before serving, heat oven; fill shell, following recipe from Step 5. Or, bake quiche early in day; let cool and refrigerate. Reheat in moderate oven (350°) for 30 minutes.
Prebake pastry shell at 450° for 8 minutes. Bake quiche at 450° for 15 minutes, then at 350° for 15 minutes.
Makes 8 servings.

1 **package piecrust mix**
1 **pound zucchini, shredded (2 cups)**
¼ **cup (½ stick) butter or margarine**
5 **sweet Italian sausages (½ pound)**
4 **ounces Swiss cheese, shredded (1 cup)**
4 **eggs**
1 **cup milk**
½ **cup heavy cream**
¼ **cup grated Parmesan cheese**
½ **teaspoon salt**
¼ **teaspoon white pepper**

1. Preheat oven to 450°. Prepare piecrust mix following label directions. Roll out to a 14-inch round on a lightly floured surface; fit into a 10-inch (6-cup) fluted quiche dish (or use a 10-inch pie plate). Trim pastry overhang to ½ inch; turn under and flute to make a stand-up edge. Prick shell well over entire surface with a fork.
2. Bake in a preheated hot oven (450°) for 8 minutes; remove to wire rack; cool slightly.
3. Sauté zucchini in 2 tablespoons of the butter in a large skillet for 5 minutes or until tender. Remove to bowl.
4. Remove casing from 4 sausages; cut remaining sausage into ½-inch-thick rounds. Cook sausage in remaining 2 tablespoons butter in same skillet until no pink remains. Drain on paper toweling.

5. Spread cooked zucchini evenly over bottom of pastry shell; sprinkle crumbled sausage and Swiss cheese over zucchini.
6. Beat eggs lightly in a large bowl. Add milk, heavy cream, cheese, salt and pepper; blend well. Pour into pastry shell. Arrange sausage rounds around edge of quiche, pressing down slightly.
7. Bake in a preheated hot oven (450°) for 15 minutes; lower oven temperature to moderate (350°) and bake 15 minutes or until center is almost firm but still soft. Let stand 15 minutes before serving.

SUGAR-FROSTED GREEN AND RED GRAPES

Makes 8 servings.

1 **bunch seedless red grapes (about 1 pound)**
1 **bunch seedless green grapes (about 1 pound)**
1 **egg white, slightly beaten Granulated sugar**

1. Cut grapes into small clusters. Wash. Pat dry with paper toweling. (Grapes must be dry before coating.)
2. Beat egg white in a small bowl until foamy. Brush grapes with egg white, coating completely. Sprinkle with sugar. Place grapes on wire racks over wax paper; let stand at room temperature until they are dry to the touch.
3. Arrange grapes on a platter.

ALMOND MACAROONS

Sugar-studded, rich and crunchy.
Bake at 325° for 20 minutes.
Makes about 3 dozen cookies.

**1 can (8 ounces)
    almond paste**
**2 egg whites,
    unbeaten**
**¼ teaspoon grated
    lemon rind**
½ cup sugar
**Candied red
    cherries,
    quartered**
Sliced almonds
Sugar

1. Preheat oven to 325°. Grease a large cookie sheet; dust with flour; tap off any excess.
2. Break up almond paste with fingers into a small bowl.
3. Add egg whites and lemon rind. Beat with electric mixer at low speed until mixture is smooth and the ingredients are well blended.
4. Add sugar slowly, beating until a soft dough forms.
5. Fit a pastry bag with a large star tip tube. Fill bag with dough.
6. Pipe dough out in small mounds or drop by teaspoonfuls on prepared cookie sheet. Garnish each with candied red cherry quarter and almond slice; sprinkle with additional sugar.
7. Bake in a preheated slow oven (325°) for 20 minutes or until light golden brown. Remove to wire racks; cool completely.

NEW YEAR'S BRUNCH

Frosted Orange Juice*
Ham Empanadas*
Stuffed Eggs Mornay*
Artichoke, Celery and Pimiento Salad*
Whole Wheat Muffins   Breakfast Rolls
Cranberries Jubilee*
Herbal Tea   Coffee
*Recipe given

FROSTED ORANGE JUICE

Makes 6 servings.

Crushed ice
**6 tablespoons
    orange-flavored
    liqueur**
Orange juice

Fill large wine glasses with crushed ice. For each serving, add 1 tablespoon liqueur and fill glass with orange juice. Garnish with lime slice, orange quarter-slice and mint, if you wish.

HAM EMPANADAS

Bake at 375° for 15 minutes.
Makes 18 empanadas.

**1 cup ground
    cooked ham**
**4 green onions,
    chopped**
**1 can (4 ounces)
    diced green
    chilies, drained**
**¼ cup dairy sour
    cream**
**Sour Cream
    Pastry (recipe
    follows)**

1. Combine ham, onions, chilies and sour cream in a medium-size bowl.
2. Roll out Sour Cream Pastry on a floured surface to an ⅛-inch thickness. Cut out 4-inch rounds.
3. Preheat oven to 375°. Put 1 tablespoon ham filling on each round; moisten edge; fold to make half circles and crimp to seal. Place on cookie sheet and prick with tines of fork.
4. Bake in a preheated moderate oven (375°) for 15 minutes or until golden brown. Cool on wire rack; serve warm.

Sour Cream Pastry: Combine 1 cup *sifted* all-purpose flour and ¼ teaspoon salt in mixing bowl. Cut in ½ cup (1 stick) butter with pastry blender until crumbly. Stir in ½ cup dairy sour cream. Gather dough into a ball; wrap and refrigerate at least 1 hour.

STUFFED EGGS MORNAY

Bake at 350° for 30 minutes.
Makes 6 servings.

8 tablespoons (1 stick) butter, softened
1 teaspoon salt
½ cup all-purpose flour
Pinch cayenne
¼ teaspoon white pepper
3 cups milk, scalded
2 ounces Swiss cheese, shredded
6 tablespoons grated Parmesan cheese
12 hard-cooked eggs

½ pound mushrooms, minced
2 tablespoons chopped fresh parsley

½ teaspoon leaf tarragon, crumbled
1 cup fresh bread crumbs (2 slices)
2 tablespoons butter, melted

1. Put 4 tablespoons of the butter in the container of an electric blender with salt, flour, cayenne, pepper and 2 cups of the hot milk. Cover; whirl for 30 seconds. Pour into large saucepan; add remaining hot milk and cook over medium heat, stirring constantly, until sauce is thickened and bubbles, about 2 minutes.
2. Add Swiss cheese and 4 tablespoons of the Parmesan. Cook, stirring constantly, until cheese is melted; remove from heat; cover.
3. Cut eggs in half, lengthwise. Empty yolks into bowl; reserve the whites.
4. Heat 4 more tablespoons of the butter in a small skillet. Sauté mushrooms for about 5 minutes or until mixture is almost dry, stirring occasionally. Stir in parsley and tarragon.
5. Mash egg yolks with ½ cup of the sauce; add the mushrooms. Fill whites with the mushroom mixture.
6. Spread a thin layer of sauce in a shallow baking dish and arrange the stuffed eggs in the sauce, stuffing-side up. Spoon remaining sauce over.
7. Toss bread crumbs and remaining 2 tablespoons Parmesan with melted butter. Sprinkle over eggs.
8. Bake in a moderate oven (350°) for 30 minutes.

ARTICHOKE, CELERY AND PIMIENTO SALAD

Makes 6 servings.

1 package (9 ounces) frozen artichoke hearts, thawed
1 cup chopped celery
2 tablespoons minced green onion

2 canned pimientos, cut into strips
½ teaspoon dry mustard

½ teaspoon salt
¼ teaspoon pepper
2 tablespoons vinegar
6 tablespoons vegetable oil
Lettuce greens or watercress

1. Combine artichokes in a bowl with celery, green onion and pimientos.
2. Mix mustard, salt, pepper, vinegar and oil in small bowl or measuring cup. Pour over artichokes; toss gently; cover bowl. Marinate in refrigerator for several hours.
3. To serve: Divide into six portions on individual salad plates lined with shredded lettuce or watercress.

CRANBERRIES JUBILEE

Makes 6 servings.

¼ cup sugar
2 teaspoons cornstarch
½ teaspoon ground cinnamon
¼ teaspoon ground nutmeg
2 tablespoons water

1 can (16 ounces) whole cranberry sauce

½ cup brandy
1 quart vanilla ice cream

1. Combine sugar, cornstarch, cinnamon and nutmeg in large saucepan; blend in water. Add cranberry sauce and cook, stirring, until sauce thickens and bubbles, 1 minute.
2. When ready to serve, reheat sauce until bubbly; pour into heatproof bowl.
3. Heat brandy until bubbles appear around edge. Ignite and pour into cranberry mixture. Stir gently until flames burn out. Serve over ice cream.

New Year's Brunch: (Clockwise from top) Frosted Orange Juice, page 7; Stuffed Eggs Mornay, page 8; Artichoke, Celery and Pimiento Salad, page 8; Ham Empanadas, page 7; Cranberries Jubilee, page 8

Whether it's a college bowl game or the Super Bowl, friends gather to watch such championship games on television. They also enjoy eating on trays set up by the host or hostess in front of the set. The TV dinner was once a quick meal served solely for convenience, but it has now become a favorite way of entertaining. The big-screen televi-

---

NEW YEAR'S BOWL GAME BUFFET

Cherry Tomatoes Stuffed with Avocado Cream*
Dilled Salmon-Topped Cucumber Rounds*
Glazed Brisket of Beef*
Biscuit Squares
Cold Meat Platter: Sliced Ham, Salami, Turkey
Cheese Tray
Party Pumpernickel or Rye Bread
Marinated Vegetable Bowl
Soft Drinks   Fruit Juice   Beer
Pineapple Cream Cheese Puffs*
Chocolate Pecan Bars*
Tea   Milk   Coffee

*Recipe given

---

sions and video-cassette screenings have boosted this form of dining. The ideal food for a tray is simple, portable, served at room temperature and eaten using only a fork. We suggest a glazed beef brisket which can be made ahead and is served thinly sliced. The two desserts are delicious, finger-size, easy-to-serve sweets that are sure to score.

CHERRY TOMATOES STUFFED WITH AVOCADO CREAM

Makes about 36.

1 **medium-size ripe avocado, peeled and pitted**	¼ **teaspoon leaf basil**	**Dash liquid hot pepper seasoning**
2 **teaspoons lemon juice**	½ **package (8-ounce size) cream cheese, softened**	1½ **pints cherry tomatoes**
1 **small clove garlic**	¼ **teaspoon salt**	**Parsley sprigs**

1. Combine avocado and lemon juice in the container of an electric blender or food processor; cover and whirl until smooth. Add garlic, basil, cream cheese, salt and hot pepper seasoning; whirl until smooth. Transfer to a medium-size bowl. Refrigerate mixture until stiff enough to pipe into tomatoes.
2. While avocado cream is chilling, cut a very thin slice off tops of tomatoes; scoop out. Drain upside down on paper toweling.
3. Fit a pastry bag with a rosette tip; fill with avocado mixture; pipe mixture into tomatoes. (Or fill tomatoes with a small spoon.) Garnish tops with a small sprig of parsley.

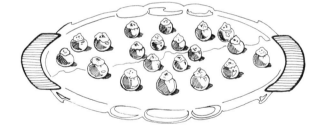

DILLED SALMON-TOPPED CUCUMBER ROUNDS

Makes about 36 rounds.

1 **can (7¾ ounces) red salmon, drained and flaked**	2 **teaspoons dillweed**	1 **teaspoon minced onion**
1 **package (8 ounces) cream cheese, softened**	1 **teaspoon grated lemon rind**	2 **cucumbers (each about 10 inches long), unpared**
	1 **teaspoon lemon juice**	**Dill sprigs**

1. Combine drained salmon, cream cheese, dillweed, lemon rind and juice and minced onion in a medium-size bowl. Beat on medium speed with electric mixer until well blended. Refrigerate until stiff enough to pipe onto cucumber rounds.
2. While mixture is chilling, score cucumbers with the tines of a fork. Cut each into eighteen ¼-inch-thick slices. Fit a star tube onto a pastry bag; fill with salmon mixture; pipe onto cucumber rounds. Garnish with a small sprig of dill.

GLAZED BRISKET OF BEEF

Makes about 20 servings.

1 **brisket of beef (about 6 to 7 pounds)**	¼ **cup firmly packed light brown sugar**	1 **tablespoon dry mustard**
1 **medium-size onion, quartered**		½ **cup chili sauce**
2 **celery stalks with leaves**		
2 **bay leaves**		
6 **peppercorns**		
¼ **cup dry sherry**		

1. Day before: Combine brisket of beef, onion, celery, bay leaves and peppercorns in a large kettle or Dutch oven; add cold water to cover meat. Bring to boiling; lower heat; cover; simmer 3 to 4 hours or until meat is fork-tender. Cool meat in broth, then remove and refrigerate.
2. Cut off any excess fat. Place beef on rack over broiler pan; pour dry sherry over meat. Sprinkle sugar and mustard evenly over top, then drizzle with chili sauce.
3. Broil 3 to 4 inches from heat for 5 minutes or until nicely glazed. Cut meat into thin slices; serve hot or warm.

PINEAPPLE CREAM CHEESE PUFFS

Easy-to-make puffs hold a tempting filling.
Bake at 400° for 40 minutes.
Makes 8 servings.

¾ **cup water**	½ **cup heavy cream**	⅓ **cup flaked coconut**
6 **tablespoons butter or margarine**	3 **tablespoons 10X (confectioners') sugar**	**10X (confectioners') sugar**
1 **teaspoon sugar**		
¼ **teaspoon salt**		
¾ **cup** *sifted* **all-purpose flour**		
3 **eggs**		
2 **cans (8 ounces each) crushed pineapple in pineapple juice**		
1 **package (8 ounces) cream cheese**		

1. Heat water, butter, sugar and salt in a medium-size saucepan to a full boil.
2. Add flour all at once. Stir vigorously with a wooden spoon until mixture forms a thick smooth paste that leaves side of pan clean, about 1 minute. Remove from heat; cool slightly.
3. Preheat oven to 400°. Add eggs, 1 at a time, beating well after each addition, until paste is smooth.
4. Drop paste by rounded tablespoonsful into 8 even mounds, 2 inches apart, on an ungreased large cookie sheet.
5. Bake in a preheated hot oven (400°) for 40 minutes or until puffed and golden brown. Remove to wire rack; cool completely.
6. Make filling: Drain juice from pineapple, reserving 4 tablespoons. Soften cream cheese in medium-size bowl. Beat in reserved pineapple juice until smooth; stir in pineapple. Beat cream with 10X sugar in a small bowl until stiff. Fold whipped cream and coconut into cream cheese.
7. Cut a slice from top of each puff; remove any filaments of soft dough. Spoon filling into puffs, dividing evenly; replace tops. Just before serving, sift 10X sugar over each puff.

CHOCOLATE PECAN BARS

Bake at 350° for 40 minutes.
Makes 24 bar cookies

1½ **cups** *sifted* **all-purpose flour**	1 **cup dark corn syrup**	1 **teaspoon vanilla**
½ **teaspoon ground cinnamon**	¼ **cup all-purpose flour**	¼ **teaspoon salt**
¼ **teaspoon baking powder**	2 **squares semi-sweet chocolate, melted and cooled**	1½ **cups pecans, coarsely chopped**
½ **cup firmly packed light brown sugar**		
¾ **cup (1½ sticks) butter, softened**		
3 **eggs**		
½ **cup firmly packed light brown sugar**		

1. Preheat oven to 350°.
2. Sift the 1½ cups flour, cinnamon and baking powder into a large bowl; stir in the ½ cup brown sugar. Cut in butter with a pastry blender until mixture is crumbly. Pat into a greased 13 × 9 × 2-inch baking pan.
3. Bake in a preheated moderate oven (350°) for 10 minutes. Remove to wire rack. Leave oven on.
4. Beat eggs, remaining brown sugar, syrup, remaining flour, chocolate, vanilla and salt in a large bowl with an electric mixer until blended. Pour over dough layer in baking pan. Sprinkle with chopped nuts.
5. Return to oven and bake 30 minutes longer. Cool on wire rack. Cut into bars.

VALENTINE'S DAY

ENJOY A CANDLELIT DINNER
AND GIVE A PARTY FOR THE KIDS.

The glow of candlelight, a bottle of your favorite wine, a fabulous gourmet dinner with someone you care about—that's the way to celebrate Valentine's Day. And when you're the one who makes the meal, it's even more special. The dinner menu here was planned so you don't have to spend much time in the kitchen. The potatoes, hollandaise sauce, frozen dessert and cakes can all be made the day before. As for the rest of the menu, it won't take more than 15 minutes to cook. If your favorite Valentine has a sweet tooth, you've probably noticed that chocolates and even Valentine cards have become quite expensive. If you have more time than money, you might try making your own cookie Valentine cards. The edible cards are

---

VALENTINE DINNER FOR TWO

Cheese, Fruit and Crackers
Steak Burgundy*
Asparagus with Hollandaise Sauce*
Herb-Sautéed Cherry Tomatoes*
Potato Cakes Cordon Bleu*
Mixed Green Salad
Cassata d'Amore*
Sweetheart Cakes*
Wine   Coffee

*Recipe given

---

not only lovely to look at, but good to eat as well. They're a cinch to make so the kids can have fun helping you. Start with our recipe for a rich sugar cookie dough, then cut it into heart shapes and rectangles that you hinge together with red ribbon after baking. Decorate with frosting or write a special message or the recipient's name. These whimsical cookie Valentines make ideal party favors for a children's Valentine party. Most children's party menus consist of cake, ice cream and punch—generally all sweet foods. In our menu, aside from the cookies, we have included recipes for nutritious foods that taste great and are fun for kids to help you make. Plan to have the party right after school when the kids are good and hungry!

STEAK BURGUNDY

Makes 2 servings.

½ teaspoon pepper
1 tablespoon olive or vegetable oil
2 individual boneless steaks (shell or club), cut ½- to ¾-inch thick
2 tablespoons butter or margarine

2 tablespoons finely chopped shallots
1 teaspoon Worcestershire sauce
2 teaspoons Dijon mustard
½ teaspoon salt

½ cup red Burgundy wine
2 tablespoons brandy
1 tablespoon chopped fresh parsley
1 tablespoon chopped chives

1. Rub pepper and oil on both sides of steaks; heat heavy skillet slowly to very hot. Add steaks to sear quickly on both sides, about 30 seconds on each side. Remove to a plate.
2. Remove skillet from heat; add butter. When melted, stir in shallots; return to heat and sauté, stirring constantly, 2 minutes. Add Worcestershire, mustard and salt. Return steaks to skillet; cook 2 minutes on each side. Remove to heated serving plate. Keep warm.
3. Add wine to skillet; cook rapidly, uncovered, until reduced by half. Stir in brandy, parsley and chives; simmer 2 minutes. Spoon a little sauce over each steak and pass remaining sauce.

ASPARAGUS WITH HOLLANDAISE SAUCE

Makes 2 servings.

2 egg yolks
2 tablespoons lemon juice
1 tablespoon hot water
½ cup (1 stick) butter or margarine
¼ teaspoon salt
Dash cayenne
¾ to 1 pound asparagus
OR: 1 package (10 ounces) frozen asparagus spears

1. To prepare Hollandaise Sauce: Beat egg yolks in a small saucepan with wooden spoon until smooth; blend in lemon juice and water. Place over low to medium heat.
2. Cut butter into 8 pieces. Add 1 piece at a time, stirring constantly until butter has been absorbed into the yolk mixture and sauce is thickened. Remove from heat; season with salt and cayenne.
3. Wash asparagus well; snip off little green scales with the tip of a knife and wash again.

4. Place stalks in boiling water in a large skillet. Cook, covered, 8 to 10 minutes or just until tender. To cook frozen asparagus, follow label directions. Drain; place on heated platter. Spoon some of Hollandaise Sauce over and pass remaining sauce.
Note: Hollandaise Sauce may be made the day ahead, refrigerated, then served at room temperature.

HERB-SAUTÉED CHERRY TOMATOES

Makes 2 servings.

1 tablespoon butter or margarine

12 to 16 cherry tomatoes, washed

¼ teaspoon salt
¼ teaspoon leaf basil, crumbled

Heat butter in small skillet; add tomatoes, salt and basil; cook, stirring often, over medium heat until heated through and skins start to split, about 5 minutes.

POTATO CAKES CORDON BLEU

Makes 2 to 4 servings.

- 3 small potatoes (¾ pound)
- 1 egg
- ¼ cup shredded Swiss cheese
- 1 small onion, grated (2 tablespoons)
- 1 tablespoon flour
- ¼ teaspoon salt
- ⅛ teaspoon pepper
- 2 tablespoons butter or margarine

1. Pare potatoes; shred directly into large bowl of cold water. Drain; rinse in cold water. Squeeze firmly in paper toweling to remove as much of the water as possible.
2. Beat egg in medium-size bowl until frothy. Add potatoes, cheese, onion, flour, salt and pepper; stir to blend.
3. Heat butter in large skillet. Drop potato mixture by rounded tablespoonsful into hot butter. Brown on one side 5 to 6 minutes; turn and brown slowly on the other side about 8 minutes or until cooked through. If you are making the day ahead, wrap in foil and refrigerate, then reheat.

CASSATA D'AMORE

Makes 6 servings.

- 1 pint vanilla ice cream
- 1 pint raspberry sherbet
- ½ cup heavy cream
- 3 tablespoons crushed amaretti cookies
- 3 tablespoons cherry preserves
  Whipped cream
  Sweetheart Cakes (recipe follows)

1. Place a 4- or 5-cup mold or bowl in freezer.
2. Soften vanilla ice cream slightly in a chilled bowl; beat until smooth but not melted. Press evenly inside chilled mold to line mold completely. Freeze until firm.
3. Soften raspberry sherbet slightly; beat until smooth. Press evenly over vanilla ice cream layer. Freeze until firm.
4. Beat heavy cream until stiff; fold in cookie crumbs and cherry preserves. Spoon into center of mold; smooth top. Freeze until firm.
5. To unmold and decorate: Remove mold from freezer; let stand 5 minutes. Invert onto serving plate. Hold a hot, damp dishcloth over mold and shake to release. Return to freezer until surface is firm.
6. Decorate around base with rosettes of whipped cream, Sweetheart Cakes and green leaves.

SWEETHEART CAKES

Makes six 2-inch cakes.

- 12 slices (¼- to ⅓-inch thick) frozen pound cake, thawed
- 3 tablespoons finely chopped walnuts
- 2 to 3 tablespoons raspberry preserves
- 1 tablespoon kirsch or cream sherry
- 1½ cups 10X (confectioners') sugar
- 4 teaspoons water
- 4 teaspoons light corn syrup
- ¼ teaspoon almond extract
- 1 to 2 drops red food coloring

1. Using a 2-inch heart-shaped cookie cutter, cut heart-shapes from cake slices.
2. Combine walnuts with enough of the preserves to make a thick paste. Sandwich cakes together by pairs with nut-jam filling; brush tops with kirsch or sherry.
3. Combine 10X sugar, water and corn syrup in medium-size bowl over barely simmering water. Heat, stirring often, until frosting is fluid and pourable. Remove from heat; reserve about 2 tablespoons for decorating. Stir almond extract and food coloring into remaining frosting to tint pink. Space filled cakes 1 inch apart on wire rack set over wax paper.
4. Pour pink frosting over cakes to cover tops and sides completely. Let dry, then pipe reserved white frosting through a writing tip in designs on top of cakes. When frosting is dry, place cakes on a plate; cover and refrigerate.

Valentine Dinner for Two: Steak Burgundy, page 13; Asparagus with Hollandaise Sauce, page 13; Herb-Sautéed Cherry Tomatoes, page 13; Potato Cakes Cordon Bleu, page 15; Sweetheart Cakes, page 15

No one knows for sure who St. Valentine was although Valentine's Day has been observed since the Middle Ages. There were at least three, some say eight, Valentines who had February 14 as his feast day, according to early records. Various legends have evolved through the ages. In one account, St. Valentine was a Roman priest, another a bishop, both of whom were martyred by

---

VALENTINE'S DAY KIDS' PARTY

Pretzel-Cheese Squares*
Honey-Nutters*
Crunchy Curls*
Pat-A-Pizzas*
Valentine Cookie Cards and Hearts*
Strawberry Milk Punch
*Recipe given

---

an emperor for refusing to give up Christianity. According to another legend, Valentine was imprisoned and fell in love with the jailer's little daughter who had become his friend. He left her a farewell note and signed it "from your Valentine." Today, Valentine's Day is the one day when kids, moms and dads, friends and lovers, express affection through flowers, candy and cards.

PRETZEL-CHEESE SQUARES

Makes 12 snacks.

12 thin pretzel sticks Unsliced American,	Cheddar, or other bar cheese cut in twelve ½-inch squares	Insert a pretzel stick into each cheese square. Place on a serving plate.

HONEY-NUTTERS

Makes 82 snacks.

1 cup chunky peanut butter
⅔ cup honey
½ cup instant nonfat dry milk powder
16 graham crackers
1 cup shredded coconut or toasted wheat germ

1. Combine peanut butter, honey and milk in a mixing bowl; stir until blended. Crush graham crackers between 2 large sheets of wax paper with a rolling pin or whirl in container of electric blender, 5 at a time, to make fine crumbs.

2. Add crumbs to the peanut butter mixture; mix with your hands until well blended.

3. Spread the coconut on wax paper. Make little balls by scooping out a teaspoonful of the peanut-butter mixture and rolling it between the palms of your hands. Roll each ball in coconut to coat evenly and serve on a party platter.

CRUNCHY CURLS

Makes 20 snacks.

2 long, thick carrots
1 cup sweet gherkins or 20 cherry tomatoes
½ cup dairy sour cream
⅛ teaspoon celery or onion salt

1. Clean and trim carrots with vegetable parer and knife. To make carrot curls, run the vegetable parer down the side of the carrot from top to bottom, pressing down firmly. Make 20 long strips at least ½-inch wide. Roll each carrot strip around your index finger to form a curl; drop curls into a bowl of ice cubes and water to keep them crisp and curled.

2. Cut pickles into chunks about 1-inch long. Unroll a carrot curl and place a pickle piece or cherry tomato (use both, if you wish) at one end. Re-roll the carrot around the filling and insert toothpick into carrot and filling. Chill well.

3. For a dip, mix sour cream with celery or onion salt in a small bowl. Cover and chill until serving time.

Valentine's Day Kids' Party: Valentine Cookie Cards and Hearts, page 18

PAT-A-PIZZAS

Bake at 425° for 10 minutes.
Makes 10 servings.

1 tablespoon butter or margarine	1 can (7.5 ounces) refrigerated biscuits (10 biscuits)	1 package (8 ounces) mozzarella or Muenster cheese	¾ cup spaghetti sauce or pizza sauce	Leaf oregano Garlic powder

1. Preheat oven to 425°. Grease a large cookie sheet with butter. Pat or roll each biscuit into a circle about 4 inches across on a cutting board. Transfer biscuits to prepared cookie sheet. (Dip fingers into flour to make it easier to pat out biscuits.)

2. Shred cheese onto wax paper. Spread 1 tablespoon of sauce on each biscuit and top with cheese. Sprinkle with a little oregano and garlic powder.

3. Bake in a preheated hot oven (425°) for about 10 minutes until the cheese is bubbly and the crust is lightly browned.

VALENTINE COOKIE CARDS AND HEARTS

Bake at 375° for 7 to 9 minutes.
Makes six 5 × 7-inch cookie cards and about twelve 1- to 4-inch cookie hearts.

3 cups *sifted* all-purpose flour
1 teaspoon baking powder
½ teaspoon salt
⅔ cup (1½ sticks) butter or margarine
¾ cup sugar
2 eggs
1 teaspoon vanilla
Red or orange sour ball candies, crushed
Royal Frosting *(recipe follows)*
Red and green food coloring

1. Sift flour, baking powder and salt onto wax paper.
2. Beat butter with sugar in large bowl with electric mixer until light and fluffy. Beat in eggs and vanilla.
3. Gradually stir in flour mixture at low speed or with wooden spoon until dough is very stiff. If needed, stir in more all-purpose flour. Wrap dough in plastic wrap; chill overnight.
4. Preheat oven to 375°. Roll out dough, one quarter at a time, between a lightly floured sheet of foil and a sheet of wax paper, to ⅛-inch-thick rectangle, lifting paper frequently to dust with flour and turning dough over for even rolling.
5. Remove wax paper. Cut dough with a pastry wheel or knife into a 5 × 7-inch rectangle. Cut rectangle crosswise in half if a small folding card is desired. Cut out heart shapes with floured cutters in various sizes within the rectangle or in dough around the rectangle. Remove dough trimmings from foil; reroll together at the end.
6. Place foil with cut-out dough on cookie sheet. Sprinkle cut-out heart shapes with candies. For a cookie heart within a candy heart, cut a large heart, then a smaller heart in the center of that heart. Remove dough around small heart; sprinkle with candies.
7. If an imprinted or pressed design is desired, use a fork or a mallet and press into dough to obtain a textured or waffled effect. If you want to tie cookie cards together, make 2 small holes in each cookie with plastic drinking straw along edges.
8. Bake in a preheated moderate oven (375°) for 7 to 9 minutes, longer for larger cookies, or until cookies are light brown and candy has melted. Remove cookies on foil to wire rack; cool completely. Gently loosen cookies from foil; store in airtight container until ready to decorate.
9. Prepare Royal Frosting. Remove some frosting into two small custard cups; tint one pink and the other green with food coloring. Spoon frosting into wax paper cone fitted with a plain writing or small star tip. Pipe decorative borders with white or colored frosting or write a special message on outside and inside of cards or hearts. Or, set smaller cookie hearts on top of larger ones with frosting in between to hold in place before decorating. When frosting is dry, tie cards with ribbon or wrap in plastic wrap for giving.

Royal Frosting: Combine 2 egg whites, ¼ teaspoon cream of tartar and ¼ teaspoon vanilla in small bowl; beat with electric mixer at high speed until foamy. Gradually beat in 3½ cups *sifted* 10X sugar until frosting stands in firm peaks and is stiff enough to hold a sharp line when cut through with a knife. Keep frosting covered with damp paper toweling to keep from drying. Makes enough frosting to decorate 6 large cookies and 12 small cookies.

CELEBRATE ST. PATRICK'S DAY

FOR A BIT OF IRISH CHARM.

Whether March comes in as a lamb or a lion, it doesn't matter to the Irish. Only one thing is sure: On the 17th of the month, the lads and lasses will celebrate with marching bands and conviviality. This is the day the Irish commemorate their patron saint who, according to legend, died at Saul, Ireland, on March 17, 492, at about the age of 106. St. Patrick introduced Christianity to Ireland. He established churches and schools. In teaching his converts about his God, St. Patrick held up a shamrock and showed them that the three-sectioned leaf represented the Father, the Son and Holy Spirit. Thus, the origin of wearing a shamrock on St. Patrick's Day. Tales of St. Patrick's miracles abound— among them, the expulsion of all the snakes from

---

ST. PATRICK'S DAY MEAL

Creamy Watercress and Leek Soup*
Oven-Glazed Corned Beef*
Boiled Cabbage Wedges
Parslied Whole Potatoes
Buttered Carrots
Emerald Mixed Green Salad
Beer
Apple Cake
Irish Coffee*

*Recipe given

Ireland. In America, the earliest celebration of this holiday was 1737 in Boston by an Irish society. This day is filled with parades and simple but hearty fare. Nothing goes better with the wearin' of the green than corned beef and cabbage. You don't have to be Irish to enjoy this popular dish on St. Patrick's Day. In fact, corned beef didn't come from the Emerald Isle. The dish was concocted by Irish immigrants when they came to America because it was inexpensive and delicious. Our updated version can be simmered the day before. Just before serving, it is brushed with a mustard sauce and glazed in the oven. It wouldn't be an Irish meal without leeks so we have included a creamy leek soup. May all good luck be with you!

CREAMY WATERCRESS AND LEEK SOUP

Makes 6 servings.

1 cup sliced washed leeks
3 tablespoons butter
4 cups water
2 medium-size potatoes, pared and sliced
1 small onion, chopped (¼ cup)
2 tablespoons minced fresh parsley
1 bay leaf
1 teaspoon salt
¼ teaspoon pepper
1 bunch watercress
1 cup heavy cream
Croutons
Chopped fresh parsley

1. Sauté leeks in butter in a large saucepan until soft but not brown, about 5 minutes.
2. Add water, potatoes, onion, parsley, bay leaf, salt and pepper. Bring to boiling; lower heat; cover. Simmer 30 minutes or until potatoes are soft. Discard bay leaf.
3. Wash and dry watercress; remove leaves. (You should have about 1 cup.) Add to potato mixture. Cook 5 minutes.
4. Puree soup, part at a time, in an electric blender. Chill several hours. Stir in cream. Serve with croutons and additional chopped fresh parsley.

OVEN-GLAZED CORNED BEEF

Bake at 350° for 30 minutes.
Makes 10 servings.

1 corned beef brisket (about 5 pounds)
2 onions
6 whole cloves
6 peppercorns
2 large bay leaves
2 cloves garlic, peeled
⅓ cup firmly packed brown sugar
1 tablespoon Dijon mustard

1. Place corned beef in kettle; cover with cold water. Bring to boiling; drain water. Cover meat with fresh cold water. Stud onions with the whole cloves; add to corned beef with peppercorns, bay leaves and garlic cloves. Cover kettle; bring to boiling; lower heat. Simmer (do not boil) 4 hours or until meat is very tender.
2. Allow meat to cool slightly in the cooking liquid; remove to shallow pan. Cover meat with another shallow pan; weight with several large books or something of a similar weight. This will ensure neat slices. Refrigerate meat with weights in place, if possible. Otherwise, leave under weights for 1 hour, then wrap; refrigerate overnight.
3. About 1 hour before serving, remove corned beef from refrigerator. Place in a shallow roasting pan. Combine brown sugar with mustard to make a smooth paste; spread over top (fat) surface of meat.
4. Bake in a moderate oven (350°) for 30 minutes or until meat is hot and glaze is bubbly and brown. Cut into thin slices across the grain. Serve with steamed cabbage wedges, small parslied potatoes and buttered carrots, if you wish.

IRISH COFFEE

Makes 8 servings.

8 teaspoons sugar
6 cups strong hot coffee
8 jiggers Irish whiskey
½ cup heavy cream, whipped

1. Heat each goblet or mug by putting a metal spoon in the empty goblet and pouring hot water onto the spoon and then into the goblet. Pour out water.
2. Put a teaspoon of sugar in each goblet. Add enough coffee to dissolve the sugar; stir. Add a jigger of Irish whiskey to each goblet, then fill goblet to within an inch of the brim with more coffee.
3. Add whipped cream by sliding each spoonful over the back of a teaspoon held over the goblet of coffee. Do not stir. Serve at once.

St. Patrick's Day Meal: Oven-Glazed Corned Beef, page 20

PASSOVER

CELEBRATED WITH SONGS AND FOODS.

Passover is a solemn but joyous eight day festival occurring in early spring. It celebrates the escape of the Jews from bondage in Egypt. They fled so quickly that the women did not have time to allow their bread to rise, and so it baked flat and crisp. This flat, crisp, unleavened bread, matzo, is a Passover staple. The first two nights of Passover are the times when family and friends gather and share long, leisurely dinners, called Seders, when the story of the Passover is retold in narrative, song and prayer. Classic fare at the Seder begins with chicken soup with matzo balls or dumplings, and often ends with a golden, sponge or nut cake. During Passover, foods must adhere to strict dietary regulations. Almost all of the Jewish holidays have their special foods, symbolic of

---

PASSOVER FOODS

Matzo Balls*
with Chicken Soup*
Duckling with Orange Sauce
Tsimmes*
Potato Latkes
Kosher Dry Table Wine
Passover Nut Cake*

*Recipe given

---

some aspect of the event being commemorated. Lamb was the sacrifice at the first Passover and lamb's blood was used to mark the houses of the Jews so that the angel of death would pass them over and they could flee from Egypt. At today's Seders, a roasted lamb shank is used to symbolize the ordeal. Jewish law forbids the use of any food containing "chometz"—wheat, rye, barley or oats that came in contact with water for 18 minutes or more during Passover. Instead, matzo meal, a flour substitute, is used. Only foods certified "kosher for Passover" by a rabbi may be used. Supermarkets usually provide their Jewish customers with a kosher food section as the holiday approaches. Here are some recipes for traditional Passover dishes.

MATZO BALLS
(Knaidlach)

Makes about 12 balls.

1 cup boiling water
1 cup matzo meal
2 tablespoons rendered chicken fat
1 egg, slightly beaten
1 teaspoon salt

1 teaspoon chopped fresh parsley
Dash pepper

Dash ground nutmeg
Chicken Soup (recipe follows)

1. Combine water and matzo meal in a medium-size bowl; stir with a fork until water is absorbed. Stir in chicken fat; add egg, salt, parsley, pepper and nutmeg; stir to mix well. Chill 1 hour.
2. Heat Chicken Soup to boiling in a large saucepan. Shape matzo mixture by rounded tablespoonfuls into balls; drop into boiling soup; lower heat; simmer, uncovered, for 20 minutes. Serve at once.

CHICKEN SOUP

Makes 2½ quarts.

1 broiler-fryer (about 3 pounds), cut up
1 marrow bone (1½ to 2 pounds)
3 quarts cold water
1 tablespoon salt
2 celery stalks with tops, sliced (1 cup)

1 sprig parsley
2 carrots, pared and sliced (1 cup)

2 onions, peeled
¼ teaspoon pepper
⅛ teaspoon ground nutmeg

1. Place chicken and marrow bone in a large saucepan or kettle; add water.
2. Bring slowly to boiling; skim; add salt; lower heat. Simmer, covered, 45 minutes. Tie celery tops and parsley together with string. Add to soup with carrots, celery and onions.
3. Simmer 45 minutes longer or until chicken is tender and falls off the bones. Remove meat and vegetables from broth; discard the bundle of greens, bone and onions.
4. Strain broth through cheesecloth into a saucepan. Skim off fat. Add pepper and nutmeg. Serve carrots and celery in the broth, if you wish. Use cooked chicken for salad or croquettes.

TSIMMES

Makes 6 servings.

8 large carrots (about 2 pounds), pared and sliced
½ cup honey
¼ cup sugar
¼ cup vegetable oil

1 teaspoon grated lemon rind

½ teaspoon salt
¼ teaspoon ground ginger

1. Cook carrots, covered, in boiling water to cover, in a large skillet, 10 minutes; drain. Add honey, sugar and oil.
2. Cook, uncovered, over low heat, stirring occasionally until carrots are tender and richly glazed, about 20 minutes. Stir in lemon rind, salt and ginger.

PASSOVER NUT CAKE

Bake at 325° for 40 minutes.
Makes 9 servings.

5 eggs, separated
⅔ cup sugar
1½ tablespoons vegetable oil
5 tablespoons matzo meal
2 tablespoons grated lemon rind

1 cup walnuts, finely chopped

10X (confectioners') sugar

1. Grease bottom of a 9×9×2-inch baking pan; line with wax paper; grease paper.
2. Beat egg yolks in small bowl of electric mixer at high speed until thick and lemon-colored. Add sugar and continue beating until thick and creamy, about 2 minutes. Stir in oil, matzo meal and lemon rind.
3. Preheat oven to 325°. Beat egg whites in large bowl until stiff but not dry; fold into yolk mixture. Fold in walnuts; pour batter into prepared pan.
4. Bake in a preheated slow oven (325°) for 40 minutes or until cake tester inserted in center of cake comes out clean.
5. Cool in pan 10 minutes; loosen around edges with a knife; turn out onto wire rack; remove wax paper; cool completely. Sprinkle with 10X sugar.

IN THE EASTER TRADITION

THIS OCCASION FEATURES BREADS, LAMB AND HAM.

Easter is a joyous holiday celebrated by Christians around the world. It is a commemoration of the resurrection of Christ and includes many festivities that originated with the pagan rites of spring dedicated to Eostre, the goddess of light. The rabbit and the egg—her fertility symbols—remain with us today. Bunnies, eggs and marshmallow chicks are only a few of the delightful traditions of Easter. Another is the serving of sweet breads. For Easter brunch, serve one of these traditional breads. We have included our favorite recipes for egg-studded Portuguese Easter breads, a lovely Easter dove bread, and perhaps the most loved Easter confection, the Babka. This is a Polish cake of which there are almost as many variations as there are bakers! We've also included our recipe for hot cross buns. The ancient Saxons sacrificed a sacred ox or "boun" to the goddess of light during their spring rites. The tradition was later modified by symbolizing the sacrifice with a small cake marked to represent the horns of the ox. Early Christians stylized this in the oldest of Easter breads, the hot cross bun, which has since made its way around the world. Our spring time lamb menu features a roast leg of lamb with artichokes that is Greek in origin, flavored with oregano and garlic. An especially good accompaniment is rice with raisins and pine nuts. Honey cake makes a sweet ending to a festive meal. The traditional ham doesn't have to look and taste the same every time. Our version is flavored and adorned with lemon and ginger—bits of which are tucked deep down in little pockets cut into the meat, while lemon slices, candied lemon rind and ginger are used for garnish. With any of our Easter menus, your day will surely be a memorable one.

EASTER BRUNCH

Fresh Fruit Compote
Scrambled Eggs
Sausages
Portuguese Easter Breads*
Hot Cross Buns*
OR
Easter Dove*
OR
Babka*
OR

Preserves	*Sweet Butter*
Coffee	*Hot Tea*

*Recipe given

PORTUGUESE EASTER BREADS

These little breads are baked with whole eggs on top for good luck, held in place by criss-crossed strips of dough.
Bake at 350° for 30 minutes.
Makes 12 individual breads.

1¼ cups very warm milk
1 cup sugar
½ cup (1 stick) unsalted butter or margarine, softened
1 teaspoon salt
2 envelopes active dry yeast
1 teaspoon sugar
3 eggs, well beaten
5 to 6 cups unsifted all-purpose flour
12 uncooked eggs in the shell
1 egg
1 teaspoon water

1. Combine 1 cup of the very warm milk (it should be comfortably warm when dropped on the wrist), the 1 cup sugar, butter and salt in a large bowl. Stir until most of the butter is melted.
2. Sprinkle yeast and the 1 teaspoon sugar into the remaining milk in a 1-cup measure; stir to dissolve. Let stand until bubbly and double in volume, about 10 minutes.
3. Stir beaten eggs, then yeast mixture, into the butter mixture. Beat in 5 cups of the flour, 1 cup at a time, until a soft dough forms.
4. Turn dough out onto a well-floured surface. Knead 8 to 12 minutes or until smooth and elastic. (Use only enough remaining flour necessary to prevent sticking.)
5. Place dough in a large buttered bowl, turning to bring buttered side up; cover. Let rise in a warm place, away from draft, about 1½ hours or until double in volume.
6. Punch dough down. Turn out onto a lightly floured surface. Divide into 14 equal pieces. Shape 12 of the pieces into round buns about ¾ inch thick, and place on 2 large, greased cookie sheets. Press down center of each with a tablespoon to make a hollow. Gently press an egg into each hollow.
7. Shape the remaining pieces of dough into two long thin rolls about 13 inches long; cut each piece into very thin strips about 6 inches long. Cross two over each egg, tucking ends under bun.
8. Let rise in a warm place for 45 minutes to 1 hour or until double in volume. Preheat oven to 350°. Beat the 1 egg with the 1 teaspoon water; brush dough with mixture.
9. Bake in a preheated moderate oven (350°) for 15 minutes. Cover tops of buns loosely with a sheet of aluminum foil to prevent over-browning. Bake 15 minutes longer or until golden brown and buns sound hollow when tapped with fingers. Cool on wire rack.

HOT CROSS BUNS

Bake at 375° for 18 minutes.
Makes 15 buns.

5 tablespoons unsalted butter or margarine
⅔ cup sugar
1 teaspoon salt
1 teaspoon ground nutmeg
¼ teaspoon ground cinnamon
1 cup milk, scalded
1 envelope active dry yeast
1 teaspoon sugar
¼ cup very warm water
2 eggs, separated
4 to 4½ cups unsifted all-purpose flour

⅔ cup dried currants
⅓ cup mixed candied fruits, finely minced with 1 tablespoon flour

1 egg white, lightly beaten
1 cup 10X (confectioners') sugar
2 tablespoons milk
½ teaspoon vanilla

1. Combine butter, the ⅔ cup sugar, salt, nutmeg and cinnamon in a large bowl. Pour in hot milk and stir to melt butter.
2. Sprinkle yeast and the 1 teaspoon sugar into the very warm water. ("Very warm water" should feel comfortably warm when dropped on wrist.) Stir until yeast dissolves. Let stand to proof until bubbly and double in volume, about 10 minutes.
3. Add yeast mixture to milk mixture; beat in egg yolks. Gradually stir in 2 cups of the flour. Beat egg whites until soft peaks form; stir into batter. Beat in 2 more cups of the flour.
4. Place dough in a large buttered bowl, turning over to bring buttered side up; cover. Let rise in a warm place, away from draft, 1½ hours or until double in volume.
5. Punch dough down; turn out on floured surface. Flip dough with floured hands and a metal spatula or scraper until it can be handled easily. Knead in the currants and candied fruit, a little at a time. Knead dough 8 to 10 minutes until smooth and elastic, using only enough flour necessary to keep dough from sticking.
6. Cut dough into 15 pieces; shape each into a smooth ball. Place about ½ inch apart in a buttered 13 × 9 × 2-inch baking pan; cover. Let rise in a warm place 1½ hours or until double in volume. Preheat oven to 375°. Brush with beaten egg white.
7. Bake in a preheated moderate oven (375°) for 18 minutes or until golden brown and buns sound hollow when tapped with fingers. Remove to a wire rack; cool.
8. Beat 10X sugar, milk and vanilla in a bowl until smooth; drizzle on buns to form wide crosses. Serve warm.

Easter Brunch: (Clockwise from left) Portuguese Easter Breads, page 27; Easter Dove, page 28; Babka, page 28

EASTER DOVE

Bake at 325° for 50 minutes.
Makes 1 very large bread.

1 envelope active dry yeast
1 teaspoon sugar
½ cup very warm milk
½ cup (1 stick) unsalted butter or margarine
⅔ cup sugar
1 tablespoon grated lemon rind
1½ teaspoons vanilla
¾ teaspoon salt
3 eggs
3 egg yolks
4½ to 5 cups *unsifted* all-purpose flour
¼ cup Marsala wine or sherry
4 ounces almond paste (half an 8-ounce package or can)
1 egg white, lightly beaten
1 tablespoon sugar

1. Sprinkle yeast and the 1 teaspoon sugar into the very warm milk in a 1-cup measure; stir to dissolve. ("Very warm milk" should feel comfortably warm when dropped on wrist.) Let stand to proof until bubbly and double in volume, about 10 minutes.
2. Beat the butter in a large bowl with electric mixer until it is light. Gradually beat in the ⅔ cup sugar, lemon rind, vanilla and salt. With mixer at low speed, add eggs and yolks, 1 at a time, ¾ cup of flour, the Marsala and yeast mixture. Gradually add 3¼ cups more of the flour, beating with a wooden spoon until a soft dough forms.
3. Turn dough out onto a well-floured surface. Flip and knead with floured hands and a metal spatula or scraper until it can be handled easily. Knead 8 to 12 minutes, using up to 1 cup of the remaining flour if necessary to prevent sticking, until the dough is smooth and elastic. (Dough will be soft.)
4. Place dough in a large buttered bowl, turning over to bring buttered side up; cover. Let rise in a warm place, away from draft, 1 to 1½ hours or until double in volume.

5. Punch dough down; cut in half and form into two balls. Place one ball on a large, greased cookie sheet; flatten to form a 10 × 5-inch curved oblong across the width of the sheet for the wings.
6. Roll the other ball of dough into a triangle about 14 inches high and 7 inches wide at the base for the body. Place over the wing piece to form a cross. Twist the top third of the body piece one way to form the head of the dove, and the bottom third in the opposite direction to form the tail. Pinch the top third to resemble a bird's head, neck and beak. Pull and stretch the bottom tail part out to a fan; shape, then cut deep slashes in both the tail and wings to resemble feathers.
7. Cut almond paste into tiny cubes; arrange in rows on the wings and tail, pushing firmly into dough. Cover. Let rise in a warm place until dough is not quite doubled, but has puffed nicely, 45 minutes. Preheat oven to 350°.
8. Brush dough well with the beaten egg white, then sprinkle wings and tail with sugar.
9. Bake in a preheated moderate oven (325°) for 50 minutes. Cool on wire rack.

BABKA

Bake at 350° for 50 minutes.
Makes 1 large cake.

1 envelope active dry yeast
1 teaspoon sugar
¼ cup very warm water
⅔ cup sugar
3¼ cups *sifted* all-purpose flour
¾ teaspoon salt
1 tablespoon grated lemon rind
5 egg yolks
2 eggs
½ cup light cream, warmed
1½ teaspoons vanilla
¾ cup (1½ sticks) unsalted butter, softened
¾ to 1 cup *unsifted* all-purpose flour
1 cup golden raisins
Confectioners' Icing *(recipe follows)*

1. Sprinkle the yeast and the 1 teaspoon sugar into the very warm water in a 1-cup measure; stir to dissolve. ("Very warm water" should feel comfortably warm when dropped on wrist.) Let stand to proof until bubbly and double in volume, about 10 minutes.
2. Combine the sugar, flour, salt and lemon rind in a large bowl and make a well in the center. Beat the egg yolks and eggs in a small bowl just enough to blend. Pour eggs, yeast mixture, cream and vanilla into well. Stir the liquid ingredients gradually into the dry ingredients until mixture is smooth. Gradually beat in the softened butter.
3. Turn dough out onto a well-floured surface. Flip and knead dough with floured hands and a metal spatula or scraper, adding the ¾ to 1 cup flour, until it can be handled easily. Knead the dough 8 to 12 minutes or until smooth and elastic. (Dough will be very soft).
4. Place dough in a large buttered bowl, turning over to bring buttered side up; cover. Let rise

in a warm place, away from draft, 1½ hours or until double in volume.
5. Butter a 10-cup Turk's head or kugelhupf mold. Sprinkle with flour, tapping out excess.
6. Punch dough down. Knead in the raisins. Let dough rest 5 minutes, then shape into a rope roughly 15 × 3 inches.
7. Press dough evenly and very firmly into the prepared mold, curving it around the center tube. Cover. Let rise in a warm place until dough reaches nearly to the top of the mold, 1 to 1½ hours. Preheat oven to 350°.
8. Bake in a preheated moderate oven (350°) for 50 minutes or until cake is nicely browned and sounds hollow when tapped with fingers.
9. Turn out onto wire rack to cool. Spoon Confectioners' Icing slowly over slightly warm cake to cover completely. Let cake cool until icing has set.
Confectioners' Icing: Combine 2 cups 10X (confectioners') sugar, 2 tablespoons rum, 2 tablespoons lemon juice and 1 tablespoon water in a small bowl; stir until smooth.

SPRINGTIME LAMB MENU

*Shrimp Bisque**
*Roast Leg of Lamb with Artichokes**
*Pine Nut and Raisin Rice**
Sautéed Green Beans
Spinach Salad with Yogurt Dressing
*Honey Cake**
Espresso

*Recipe given

SHRIMP BISQUE

A creamy, delicate shellfish soup with a light touch of wine. The bisque can be made early in the day through step 2 and then stored in the refrigerator.
Makes 8 servings.

- ½ cup (1 stick) butter
- 1 medium-size carrot, thinly sliced
- 1 small onion, chopped (¼ cup)
- 1 bay leaf
- ¼ teaspoon leaf thyme, crumbled
- ½ cup dry white wine
- ¾ pound raw shrimp, shelled and deveined
- ⅓ cup all-purpose flour
- ½ teaspoon salt
- 2 to 3 teaspoons paprika
- 3 cups milk
- 2 cups half-and-half
- Fresh dill

1. Melt 2 tablespoons of the butter in a large saucepan. Sauté carrot and onion until tender, about 3 minutes. Add bay leaf, thyme, wine and shrimp. Cook just until shrimp turn pink, about 3 minutes. Drain shrimp into a bowl, reserving liquid.

2. Melt remaining 6 tablespoons butter in same saucepan; stir in flour. Cook, stirring constantly, until bubbly. Add reserved shrimp liquid to saucepan along with salt, paprika and milk. Cook, stirring constantly, until mixture thickens.

3. Reserve 8 whole shrimp; coarsely chop remainder. Add chopped shrimp and vegetables with half-and-half to saucepan; heat thoroughly. Pour into soup tureen. Garnish with reserved whole shrimp and fresh dill.

ROAST LEG OF LAMB WITH ARTICHOKES

This classic Greek way with lamb with its predominant flavors of fresh lemon and garlic is perfect for Easter dinner.
Roast at 425° for 15 minutes, then at 325° for 1 hour and 30 minutes.
Makes 8 servings.

- 1 leg of lamb (about 4½ to 5 pounds)
- 1 small lemon
- 1 to 2 cloves garlic, slivered
- Fresh dill sprigs
- 1 teaspoon salt
- ½ teaspoon leaf oregano, crumbled
- 4 artichokes
- ½ cup lemon juice
- Water
- 2 tablespoons chopped dill
- 1 teaspoon cornstarch

1. Place lamb, fat-side up, in large shallow roasting pan. Peel lemon thinly (use bright yellow rind only); cut rind into slivers. Make small slits with paring knife over surface of lamb. Insert slivers of lemon peel, garlic and a little dill in each slit. Sprinkle with salt and oregano.

2. Roast in a hot oven (425°) for 15 minutes; lower heat to moderate (325°); roast 30 minutes.

3. Trim stalk from base of artichokes; cut 1½-inch slice from tops; snip off spiky ends from remaining leaves; halve artichokes; scrape out choke; rub all surfaces with lemon juice.

4. Parboil artichokes in boiling salted water 5 minutes; drain.

5. Add artichokes to roasting pan with lamb.

Combine lemon juice, ¼ cup water and 1 tablespoon dill; drizzle over lamb and artichokes. Roast about 1 hour longer or until artichokes are tender and meat thermometer registers 175° for medium-done lamb.

6. Place roast and artichokes on platter. Keep warm.

7. Strain liquid in roasting pan into a 2-cup measure; allow to stand 5 minutes; skim off all fat. Pour liquid (there should be about 1 cup) into small saucepan; heat to boiling. Combine cornstarch with 1 tablespoon water; stir into boiling liquid. Cook, stirring constantly, until mixture thickens and bubbles 1 minute. Stir in 1 tablespoon chopped dill. Taste; add additional salt, pepper and dill, if necessary.

PINE NUT AND RAISIN RICE

Makes 8 servings.

1 medium-size onion, chopped (½ cup)	¼ cup (½ stick) butter or margarine	2 cans (13¾ ounces each) chicken broth
1 clove garlic, crushed	2 cups uncooked long-grain rice	½ cup raisins
		½ cup pine nuts

Sauté onion and garlic in butter in large skillet about 3 minutes or until tender. Add rice and chicken broth. Cover; lower heat; simmer 20 minutes or until rice is tender. Add raisins and nuts; fluff with fork.

HONEY CAKE

Bake at 300° for 1 hour and 15 minutes.
Makes one 10-inch tube cake.

1¾ cups honey
1 cup strong coffee
2 tablespoons brandy
3½ cups *unsifted* all-purpose flour
3 teaspoons baking powder
1 teaspoon baking soda
1¼ teaspoons ground cinnamon
¼ teaspoon ground cloves
¼ teaspoon ground ginger
¼ teaspoon ground nutmeg
½ cup chopped almonds
½ cup chopped raisins
1 tablespoon grated lemon rind
4 eggs
1 cup firmly packed light brown sugar
1 tablespoon vegetable oil

1. Grease a 10-inch tube pan.
2. Heat honey and coffee to boiling in a medium-size saucepan. Cool completely. Stir in brandy.
3. Preheat oven to 300°. Sift flour, baking powder, baking soda, cinnamon, cloves, ginger and nutmeg onto wax paper; add almonds, raisins and lemon rind.
4. Beat eggs slightly in a large bowl; add honey mixture, sugar and oil. Beat until smooth and completely blended. Add flour mixture and beat until batter is smooth; pour batter into prepared pan.
5. Bake in a preheated slow oven (300°) for 1 hour and 15 minutes or until center springs back when lightly pressed with fingertip.
6. Cool in pan on wire rack for 10 minutes; loosen around edges and tube with small spatula. Turn out onto wire rack to cool completely.

FESTIVE EASTER DINNER

Stuffed Eggs
Baked Lemon-Ginger Ham*
Buttered Green Beans with Onions
Asparagus à la Française*
Baby Carrots
New Potatoes with Chives
Cucumber and Lettuce Salad
Braided Poppy Seed Rolls
Rhubarb and Strawberry Soufflé*
Coffee   Wine   Tea

*Recipe given

Festive Easter Dinner: Baked Lemon-Ginger Ham, page 32

BAKED LEMON-GINGER HAM

Bake at 325° for about 3 hours.
Makes 8 servings plus leftovers.

1 **can (8¼ ounces) sliced pineapple in pineapple juice**	
1 **jar (10 ounces) ginger preserved in syrup**	
4 **lemons**	
1 **bone-in fully cooked ham (about 12 pounds)**	
1 **tablespoon cornstarch**	

1. Drain pineapple, reserving juice in saucepan. Cut slices into ½-inch pieces. Drain syrup from ginger into saucepan with pineapple juice. Shred enough ginger to measure ¼ cup.
2. Grate rind of two lemons and remove rind of other two with a vegetable parer. Combine pineapple pieces, shredded ginger and grated lemon rind in small bowl.
3. Trim any skin and excess fat from ham to leave a ¼-inch fat layer. Make deep cuts with a small paring knife about 1 inch apart in fat side of ham. Widen cuts with finger or use handle of wooden spoon; press a flavored pineapple piece into each cut. Place ham, fat-side up, in shallow roasting pan.
4. Bake in a slow oven (325°) for 15 minutes a pound or about 3 hours. About 30 minutes before ham is done, blend cornstarch into reserved juice and syrup. Cook until thickened, stirring constantly. Brush some over ham; bake 20 minutes more. Transfer to platter.
5. While ham rests 20 minutes, prepare garnish. Cut strips of lemon rind into julienne strips; boil in water several minutes; drain. Cut off all white membrane from lemons; slice. Garnish ham with sliced lemons and halved ginger, holding slices in place with halved wooden picks, if needed. Dip julienned rind in leftover glaze; sprinkle on top of ham. Tuck parsley here and there, if you wish. Surround ham on platter with cooked vegetables, if you wish.

ASPARAGUS À LA FRANÇAISE

Makes 8 servings.

3 **pounds fresh asparagus**
3 **tablespoons butter or margarine**
4 **cups shredded iceberg lettuce**
6 **sprigs parsley**
1 **tablespoon sugar**
1½ **teaspoons salt**
3 **small white onions, sliced**
and separated into rings
1 **teaspoon flour**
1 **tablespoon butter or margarine, softened**

1. Pare asparagus stalks thinly with a vegetable parer. Wash stalks well. Break off tough ends. Cut spears into 3- or 4-inch lengths.
2. Melt 3 tablespoons butter in large skillet. Add lettuce, parsley, sugar and salt. Arrange asparagus on top, keeping stalks parallel to each other. Top with onion rings. Bring to boiling; lower heat; cover. Simmer 10 minutes or until asparagus is just tender. Discard parsley.
3. Blend flour and butter to a paste; add to liquid in bottom of pan. Cook until sauce is thickened, stirring carefully so that asparagus is not tossed. Lift lettuce, then asparagus and onion rings with tongs to platter surrounding ham or serve in separate dish. Spoon pan juices on top.

RHUBARB AND STRAWBERRY SOUFFLÉ

Makes 8 to 10 servings.

4 **cups frozen unsweetened cut rhubarb (about 1 pound package), or fresh rhubarb, if available**
¾ **cup sugar**
2 **tablespoons cornstarch Dash salt**
1 **cup water**
⅓ **cup orange-flavored liqueur or juice**
1 **tablespoon lemon juice**
2 **envelopes unflavored gelatin**
½ **cup cold water**
1 **package (10 ounces) frozen sliced strawberries**
4 **large egg whites, at room temperature**
½ **cup sugar**
1 **cup heavy cream**

1. Cook rhubarb, sugar, cornstarch, salt and water until rhubarb is tender, stirring often. Stir in liqueur and juice; cook 1 minute more.
2. Remove 2 cups rhubarb mixture for sauce; chill. Soften gelatin in water. Stir into rhubarb remaining in pan; stir in strawberries. Cook until gelatin is dissolved and berries are thawed. Pour mixture into blender container. Cover; whirl until smooth. Cool slightly.
3. Beat egg whites with electric mixer in large bowl until foamy. Beat in sugar, 1 tablespoon at a time, until soft peaks form. Fold rhubarb-strawberry mixture gently into whites.
4. Beat cream in small bowl until stiff. Fold into rhubarb mixture. Pour into a glass bowl. Chill until firm. Spoon rhubarb sauce on top or serve in bowl with the soufflé.

A TREAT FOR MOM ON HER DAY

LET THE KIDS TAKE CHARGE.

Mother's Day only comes once a year, on the second Sunday in May. Let the kids and Dad take charge of the kitchen for this special day. It's a way for them to express how much they love you and care for what you have done all through the year. Here is a simple menu that 10- to 12-year-old kids can prepare with Dad. (We'll assume they've had a little practice in the kitchen.) The fruit ambrosia should be made first and placed in the refrigerator to chill while the rest of the meal is being made. The lettuce or greens should be washed and dried. The tomatoes and lettuce can

---

MOTHER'S DAY DINNER

Three-Fruit Ambrosia*
Baked Ham Steak with Sweet Potatoes*
Lettuce and Tomato Salad
A Favorite Salad Dressing
Dinner Rolls
Chocolate Ice Cream Pie*
Coffee   Milk

*Recipe given

---

be placed in a salad bowl and refrigerated until dinnertime. Mix your favorite salad dressing and refrigerate. The ham steak with sweet potatoes can be prepared next and, while it's baking, the table can be set. Heat the dinner rolls, if you wish, during the last few minutes the ham and potatoes are baking. The dessert can be made ahead so that there's no last-minute rush. The coffee can be made last. And don't forget to fill a small vase with some of Mom's favorite flowers and place it in the center of the table. Say, Mom, we hope that you had a pleasant, relaxing day off.

THREE-FRUIT AMBROSIA

Makes 6 servings.

1 can (8 ounces) sliced pineapple	1 can (11 ounces) mandarin oranges	2 tablespoons shredded coconut
1 can (16 ounces) apricot halves	¼ cup orange juice	

1. Drain pineapple, apricot halves and oranges. Cut pineapple into pieces. Combine fruit in a compote dish or bowl. Drizzle with orange juice. Sprinkle top with coconut.
2. Cover dish with plastic wrap. Refrigerate until serving time.

BAKED HAM STEAK WITH SWEET POTATOES

Bake at 375° for 30 minutes.
Makes 4 servings.

1 center-cut ham steak (about 1¼ pounds)	1 can (5½ ounces) apple juice	1 can (17 ounces) sweet potatoes, drained
8 whole cloves	1 cup firmly packed light brown sugar	

1. Stud ham steak with whole cloves. Place in shallow baking dish. Pour apple juice over meat. Sprinkle with brown sugar.
2. Bake in a moderate oven (375°) for 15 minutes. Arrange sweet potatoes around outer edge of baking dish. Spoon baking liquid over meat and potatoes.
3. Bake 15 minutes longer or until glazed.

CHOCOLATE ICE CREAM PIE

Makes 6 servings.

1 package (4 ounces) instant chocolate pudding and pie filling mix	1 cup milk	1 nine-inch chocolate crumb pie shell
	1 pint chocolate ice cream, slightly softened	Whipped cream in aerosol can

1. Combine instant pudding mix and milk in a large bowl; beat with electric mixer at low speed until blended. Increase speed to medium and beat just until thickened; turn off mixer. Add ice cream in spoonfuls; beat with mixer just until mixture is smooth.
2. Pour mixture into pie shell. Place in freezer section of refrigerator for at least 1 hour or until cold. Garnish with whipped cream just before serving.

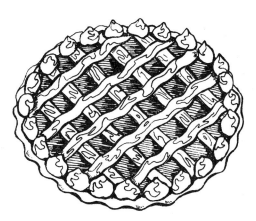

MEMORIAL DAY

BE CREATIVE WITH PICNIC FOODS.

When Memorial day arrives, it signals the beginning of glorious summer. At this time of year, the impulse to picnic is almost irresistible—whether it's at the beach, in a park, at a baseball game or tennis match, open-air concert or simply a trip to the countryside or up to the roof. Be creative when the picnic impulse hits. Rather than the typical picnic fare of fried chicken and potato salad, prepare an outdoor feast of lentil salad with chunks of frankfurters or crudités with an herb dressing. And don't forget to end your outdoor feast on a sweet note with cake and cookies. The possibilities are extremely varied, but not every food that can be enjoyed cold or at room temperature is suitable for the picnic basket. Even when food is kept and transported in a cooler, the heat eventually penetrates, especially when the cooler is opened fre-

---

COUNTRY PICNIC FARE

Stuffed Eggs
Thrice-Cooked Spareribs*
Frank and Lentil Salad*
Pasta Niçoise*
Raw Vegetables with Creamy Garlic and
Herb Dressing*
Apple Potato Salad
Apricot-Glazed Peach Cake*
Pecan Cookies*
Iced Tea   Beer

*Recipes given

---

quently to obtain drinks. On a very warm day, rapid spoilage that may cause food poisoning can result. The solution: Keep a separate cooler for beverages. Also, select foods that will not wilt or spoil en route. Dishes made with dairy products are susceptible to spoilage. Contrary to what many people think, mayonnaise-dressed salads and meats are fine for picnics. Store-bought mayonnaise has a high acid-salt level which aids in protecting the food against the growth of bacteria. However, those foods should still be kept refrigerated. Often the cause of poisoning is the mishandling of foods rather than the food itself. Cleanliness during food preparation is essential as is keeping hot foods hot and cold foods cold. The possibilities of picnic fare are limited only by your imagination, taste and appetite.

THRICE-COOKED SPARERIBS

Makes 6 servings.

1 whole rack spareribs (about 4 pounds)
¼ cup all-purpose flour
¼ cup cornstarch
6 tablespoons water
    Vegetable oil for frying
½ cup bottled steak or meat sauce
½ cup catsup
3 tablespoons sugar

1. Cut rack of ribs into individual ribs. Simmer ribs in water to cover in a large kettle for 30 minutes or until tender; drain.
2. Combine flour and cornstarch in a medium-size bowl; blend in water until smooth. Coat each rib thoroughly.
3. Pour enough oil in a deep-fat fryer or large saucepan to fill pan ½ full. Heat until temperature registers 375° on a deep-fat frying thermometer. Carefully deep-fry ribs, a few at a time, 5 minutes on each side or until crisp.

4. Remove ribs to paper toweling to drain.
5. Spoon 2 tablespoons of the oil from the fryer to a large skillet. Add meat sauce, catsup and sugar; cook over medium heat, stirring constantly, for 3 minutes or until sauce thickens. Add fried ribs; stir until ribs are thoroughly coated. Pack ribs into a toteable container; refrigerate until serving time. Serve at room temperature.

FRANK AND LENTIL SALAD

Makes 8 servings.

1½ cups dried lentils
10 cups water
1 tablespoon salt

6 frankfurters, cut into ½-inch slices

½ cup halved, pitted ripe olives
⅔ cup vegetable oil

⅓ cup red wine vinegar
1 tablespoon Dijon mustard

1 small red onion, finely chopped (¼ cup)
½ teaspoon salt
¼ teaspoon pepper

1. Rinse lentils in a colander under running cold water. Combine lentils and water in a large saucepan. Bring to boiling; add 1 tablespoon salt; lower heat; cover; simmer for 50 minutes or until tender. Drain.
2. Combine lentils, frankfurters and olives in a large toteable bowl or container; toss lightly.
3. Combine oil, vinegar, mustard, onion, ½ teaspoon salt and pepper in a small bowl, blending well. Pour over lentils; toss lightly. Cover and chill thoroughly.

PASTA NIÇOISE

Makes 8 servings.

1 package (1 pound) medium-size shell macaroni
1 package (9 ounces) frozen cut green beans, thawed

2 cans (7 ounces each) tuna, drained and flaked
1 cup halved, pitted ripe olives
1 cup vegetable oil
½ cup white wine vinegar
¼ chopped fresh parsley

1 tablespoon Dijon mustard
1 teaspoon salt
½ teaspoon pepper
8 flat anchovy fillets, drained
3 hard-cooked eggs, sliced
3 ripe tomatoes, cut into wedges

1. Cook macaroni following label directions; drain and rinse with cold water.
2. Combine macaroni, thawed green beans, tuna and olives in a large toteable bowl or container; toss lightly.
3. Combine oil, vinegar, parsley, mustard, salt and pepper in a small bowl, blending well. Pour over macaroni; toss lightly. Cover; refrigerate until cold.
4. Before toting, arrange anchovies, eggs and tomatoes on top of the salad.

RAW VEGETABLES WITH
CREAMY GARLIC AND HERB DRESSING

A great choice with a bouquet of raw vegetables.
Makes about 1½ cups dressing.

¼ **cup milk** ½ **cup mayonnaise** **or salad dressing** ½ **cup dairy sour** **cream** 2 **cloves garlic,** **halved**	1 **tablespoon** **coarsely** **chopped fresh** **parsley** ½ **teaspoon leaf** **basil** OR: 1 **tablespoon** **fresh basil**	**Raw vegetables:** **broccoli** **flowerets,** **radishes, red** **and green** **pepper strips,** **yellow squash** **chunks, turnip** **slices**

1. Combine milk, mayonnaise, sour cream, garlic, parsley and basil in container of electric blender; cover; whirl until smooth. Taste; add salt and pepper, if you wish.
2. Pour into an insulated container with a tight-fitting cover for toting. Serve with raw vegetables of your choice.

APRICOT-GLAZED
PEACH CAKE

Bake at 350° for 55 minutes.
Makes 8 servings.

2 **cups** *sifted* **all-purpose flour** 1 **cup sugar** 3 **teaspoons** **baking powder** ½ **teaspoon salt** ½ **cup (1 stick)** **butter or** **margarine,** **softened** 1 **egg**	½ **cup milk** 3 **medium-size** **peaches** 2 **tablespoons** **sugar**	½ **teaspoon ground** **cinnamon** ¼ **teaspoon ground** **nutmeg**	2 **tablespoons** **butter or** **margarine,** **melted**	1 **tablespoon** **slivered almonds** ¼ **cup apricot** **preserves**

1. Preheat oven to 350°. Sift flour, the 1 cup sugar, baking powder and salt into a large bowl; cut in the ½ cup butter until crumbly.
2. Beat egg in a small bowl until frothy; stir in milk. Pour milk mixture into flour mixture, stirring until well mixed. Spread batter in lightly greased 11 × 7 × 1½-inch baking pan.
3. Drop peaches into a saucepan of boiling water for 15 seconds; lift out with a slotted spoon. Rinse with cold water; peel, slice and pit peaches. Arrange peach slices on top of batter. Combine the 2 tablespoons sugar, cinnamon and nutmeg; sprinkle over peaches; drizzle melted butter over all.
4. Bake in a preheated moderate oven (350°) for 55 minutes or until top springs back when lightly touched with fingertip. Sprinkle almonds over top of cake. Heat apricot preserves in a small saucepan until melted; brush over top of cake. Cool on wire rack.

PECAN
COOKIES

Bake at 300° for 25 minutes.
Makes about 30 cookies.

½ **cup (1 stick)** **unsalted butter,** **softened** ½ **cup sugar** 1 **egg yolk** 1 **teaspoon almond** **extract** 1 **cup** *sifted* **all-purpose flour**	½ **cup chopped** **pecans**	**Whole pecan** **halves**

1. Grease and flour two cookie sheets. Beat butter, sugar, egg yolk and almond extract in a medium-size bowl until light and fluffy. Stir in flour and chopped pecans; mix well. Refrigerate for 30 minutes.
2. Preheat oven to 300°. Roll dough by teaspoonful between palms of hands into 1-inch balls. Place 1 inch apart on prepared cookie sheets. Press a peach half into center of each cookie.
3. Bake in a preheated slow oven (300°) for 25 minutes or until lightly browned. Cool on wire racks. Store in toteable container.

FOR FATHER'S DAY

HAVE A BACKYARD BARBECUE.

Father deserves the best and what can top steak grilled on a barbecue? Our steak recipe has a tasty Oriental sauce that gives the meat a unique flavor. Along with the steak, grill cut-up corn on the cob and ripe, juicy red tomatoes. Add the buttered crumb topping to the tomatoes just before serving. Place a loaf of French or Italian bread, spread with garlic butter and wrapped in foil, on the grill to heat while the steak cooks. A crunchy, creamy coleslaw is the perfect salad accompaniment. And for the grand finale, serve a rich, luscious blueberry cheesecake. The beauty of this dessert is that it does not have to be baked and can be made well ahead and stored in the freezer. Our other patio barbecue is just as delicious as the steak dinner. The barbecued chicken is fingerlicking good. Bake the potatoes in the coals while you're grilling the chicken. Use fresh young summer vegetables for the kabobs—cut-up zucchini, yellow squash, green and red peppers make a colorful combination. Brush the vegetables with oil or melted butter and seasonings before cooking. While the coals are low, place the foil-wrapped fruit on the grill and "bake" until tender. Since this is Dad's day, he may want to relinquish the backyard chef's job to someone else. If that's the case, here are some hints on how to grill like a pro. Use tongs to turn food rather than a fork. Brush thick or sweet sauces on food after the food has cooked until almost done. You'll serve up the best barbecued food Dad has ever had!

FATHER'S DAY STEAK BARBECUE

Sweet and Sour Curry Dip*
Cucumber, Celery and Carrot Sticks
California Barbecued Steak*
Corn on the Cob
Crumb-topped Grilled Tomatoes
Garlic Bread
Creamy Coleslaw*
Frozen Blueberry Ripple Cheesecake*
Beer   Soft Drinks   Lemonade

*Recipe given

SWEET AND SOUR CURRY DIP

A beautifully balanced sweet and sour sauce—also delicious on cold poultry, fish and seafood.
Makes about 1 cup.

1 tablespoon honey	1 tablespoon curry powder	⅛ teaspoon cayenne
1 tablespoon prepared mustard	1 cup mayonnaise	1 teaspoon lemon juice

1. Blend the honey, mustard and curry in a small bowl until smooth. Stir in mayonnaise, cayenne and lemon juice and blend until smooth.
2. Spoon into a serving bowl and serve at once or cover and refrigerate.

CALIFORNIA BARBECUED STEAK

Makes 10 servings.

1 top sirloin steak, cut 2 inches thick (about 2½ pounds) OR: 1 flank steak (about 2 pounds)	¾ cup catsup ¾ cup chili sauce 1½ tablespoons soy sauce	3 tablespoons honey 3 tablespoons hoisin sauce *(optional)*	3 tablespoons minced green onions	3 cloves garlic, mashed ½ teaspoon salt ⅛ teaspoon pepper

1. Put steak in a plastic food bag. If using flank steak, score top diagonally on both sides.
2. Combine catsup, chili sauce, soy sauce, honey, hoisin sauce, if using, green onions, garlic, salt and pepper in a small bowl; mix well. Pour mixture into bag with steak. Fasten bag securely with wire tape. Place bag in a shallow pan. Let marinate in refrigerator 24 hours, turning occasionally, if possible.
3. Lift steak out of marinade; pat with paper toweling. Broil 4 inches from heat, brushing several times with marinade, about 8 minutes on each side for rare, for the sirloin, or 5 minutes on each side for the flank steak. If grilling outdoors, grill 6 inches from grayed coals, about the same time. Serve with fresh corn on the cob and grilled tomatoes; garnish with chopped green onions and onion "brushes," if you wish.

CREAMY COLESLAW

What would a barbecue be without a big bowl of creamy coleslaw?
Makes about 8 cups.

1 large head cabbage (about 4 pounds), shredded (about 4 quarts) ¼ cup sugar	¼ cup lemon juice ¼ cup mayonnaise or salad dressing ¼ cup light cream or half-and-half	½ teaspoon salt ¼ teaspoon pepper 1 cup grated carrots ½ cup diced green pepper

1. Place shredded cabbage in a very large bowl; sprinkle with sugar; toss just until mixed; cover. Chill 30 minutes.
2. Mix lemon juice, mayonnaise and cream in a 1-cup measure; pour over cabbage. Sprinkle with salt and pepper; add carrots and green pepper; toss to mix well.

FROZEN BLUEBERRY RIPPLE CHEESECAKE

Makes 12 servings.

- **¾ cup graham cracker crumbs**
- **2 tablespoons sugar**
- **3 tablespoons butter, melted**
- **1 cup sugar**
- **⅓ cup water**
- **⅛ teaspoon cream of tartar**
- **3 egg whites**
- **2 packages (8 ounces each) cream cheese, softened**
- **½ cup dairy sour cream**
- **2 teaspoons vanilla**
- **1 tablespoon grated lemon rind**
- **½ cup blueberry preserves**
- **Whipped cream**
- **Fresh or frozen unsweetened blueberries**

1. Combine crumbs, 2 tablespoons sugar and butter in a small bowl; blend well. Press firmly over bottom of an 8-inch springform pan. Chill.
2. Combine 1 cup sugar, water and cream of tartar in a small saucepan; bring to boiling. Boil rapidly 8 to 10 minutes or until syrup registers 236° on a candy thermometer (or until syrup spins a 2-inch thread when dropped from a spoon).
3. Meanwhile, in a large bowl of electric mixer, beat egg whites until stiff peaks form; pour hot syrup in a thin stream over egg whites while beating constantly. Continue beating until very stiff peaks form and mixture cools, altogether about 15 minutes.
4. Beat cream cheese and sour cream until light and fluffy; beat in vanilla and lemon rind. Add ¼ of meringue to cheese mixture; stir to combine well. Fold remaining meringue into cheese mixture until no streaks of meringue and cheese remain.
5. Spoon about ¼ of cheese mixture into prepared pan; drizzle part of blueberry preserves over. Continue to layer cheese mixture and preserves this way. Freeze overnight or until firm.
6. To serve: Remove side of pan. Garnish top of cake with rings of whipped cream and blueberries.

BBQ CHICKEN MENU

Barbecued Chicken*
Spicy Marinated Shrimp*
Baked Potatoes
Grilled Mixed Vegetable Kabobs
Avocado, Cucumber, Lettuce Salad
Baked Apples or Pears with Syrup*
Vanilla Ice Cream
Wine   Fruit Drinks   Iced Tea

*Recipe given

BARBECUED CHICKEN

Cooking chicken before brushing it with sauce keeps it from charring too much.
Makes 8 servings.

- **2 broiler-fryers (about 3 pounds each), cut up**
- **2 teaspoons salt**
- **½ teaspoon pepper Piquant Barbecue Sauce (recipe follows)**

1. Sprinkle chicken pieces with salt and pepper. Place chicken on foil-lined grill over gray coals. Cook slowly, turning occasionally, for about 45 minutes or until almost fork-tender.
2. Remove foil from grill. Place chicken directly on grill; brush generously with Piquant Barbecue Sauce. Continue to grill, turning often and brushing with sauce until chicken is fork-tender and well glazed. Heat remaining sauce to serve with chicken.

Piquant Barbecue Sauce: Sauté 1 cup finely chopped onion and 1 clove finely chopped garlic in 3 tablespoons butter or margarine in a large saucepan until golden and tender, about 5 minutes. Stir in 1 can (16 ounces) tomato puree, ½ cup firmly packed brown sugar, ½ cup lemon juice, ½ cup bottled steak or meat sauce and 1 tablespoon salt. Bring to boiling; lower heat. Simmer, partially covered, stirring occasionally, for 20 minutes. Makes about 3¼ cups.

Overleaf: BBQ Chicken Menu: Barbecued Chicken, page 41; Spicy Marinated Shrimp, page 44; Baked Apples or Pears with Syrup, page 44

SPICY MARINATED SHRIMP

Make-ahead Note: Prepare the marinade a day or so ahead and refrigerate. Party morning: Pour marinade over the warm shrimp right in the serving bowl. Cover and refrigerate.
Makes 8 servings.

2 pounds cooked fresh shrimp, shelled and deveined but with tails left on OR: 1½ pounds cooked frozen, shelled, deveined shrimp	1 large red onion, sliced 2 large lemons, sliced ½ cup olive or vegetable oil	¼ cup wine vinegar 2 tablespoons lemon juice 1 clove garlic, halved	1 bay leaf 1 teaspoon dry mustard 1 teaspoon leaf basil, crumbled 1 teaspoon salt	¼ teaspoon black pepper 3 or 4 whole allspice Fresh parsley sprigs

1. Layer shrimp, red onion and lemon slices in a medium-size bowl.
2. Combine oil, vinegar, lemon juice, garlic, bay leaf, dry mustard, basil, salt, pepper and allspice in a jar with a tight-fitting lid; cover; shake to mix thoroughly.
3. Pour marinade over shrimp; toss gently. Cover; refrigerate several hours or overnight, tossing occasionally. Serve with decorative food picks and garnish with parsley sprigs.

BAKED APPLES OR PEARS WITH SYRUP

Warm fruit with a simple syrup is a refreshing finish for a barbecue.
Makes 8 servings.

8 large cooking apples or pears
½ cup chopped walnuts
⅓ cup raisins
⅓ cup orange marmalade
1 cup water
¼ cup (½ stick) butter or margarine
1 cup maple or maple-blended syrup
½ teaspoon ground cinnamon
½ teaspoon ground nutmeg

1. Pare apples or pears ⅓ of the way down and remove core. Combine walnuts, raisins and marmalade in small bowl. Fill cored centers of apples or pears with mixture.
2. Place each apple or pear on a square of heavy-duty foil and add 2 tablespoons of the water. Wrap and seal. Repeat with remaining apples or pears.
3. Place packages directly on coals along the sides of the grill pan; bake 40 minutes or until tender, turning packages every 10 minutes. Time will depend on size of fruit and heat of coals. To test for doneness, unwrap one package. Fruit is done when easily pierced with a fork.
4. Combine butter, syrup, cinnamon and nutmeg in a small saucepan. Heat on grill until butter is melted and syrup bubbly. Place fruit on serving plate; top each with syrup. Serve with ice cream, if you wish.

FOURTH OF JULY

AMERICANA BACKYARD FEASTS.

Celebrate our country's birthday with a rollicking picnic at the old homestead for family and close friends. Our first July 4th menu is a feast of simple but hearty foods from across the country to please all ages and appetites. Start your backyard banquet with a savory cheese tart or refreshing vegetable salad. Then there's a succulent glazed ham that's teamed up with baked beans. A chicken stew with vegetables will please all the folks. For dessert, serve luscious nectarine pie or southern cake. A sure way to get everybody into the fun and nobody tied up in a hot kitchen—after all, it's Independence Day—is to have each guest or family group bring a dish. Everyone—even the children—will feel they've pitched in. All it takes is a little planning. The result is a great time. For those who are travel-ing in, have them bring foods that carry well and can be eaten cold or at room temperature. That would include fried chicken, potato or macaroni salad, relishes, breads, cakes, pies and cookies. The host family can supply the hot foods such as grilled meats or old-fashioned churned vanilla ice cream which can be served with cake, pie or fresh berries. For a bracing summer cooler, pour glasses of lemonade with strawberries and lemon slices. When feeding a crowd, rely on a buffet service. To make sure hot foods stay hot, use warming trays and crock pots. Or, to keep cold foods chilled, set in bowls of ice. Also, plan to replenish dishes often rather than put out large quantities in the beginning. Our menus will make your celebration the best in eating!

FOURTH OF JULY FAMILY REUNION

Iowa Blue Cheese Tart*
with Fresh Fruit
Cape Cod Baked Ham*
Hot and Hearty Texas Spareribs*
Baked Beans
Carolina Brunswick Stew
Big Sur Vegetable Salad with Avocado Dressing*
Cucumber Relish*
Great Lakes Garden Salad Mold*
Mexican Corn Sticks*
Nectarine Pie
Charleston Lady Baltimore Cake*
Fruit Punch   Iced Coffee

*Recipe given

IOWA BLUE CHEESE TART

Bake at 375° for 45 minutes.
Makes 12 servings.

½ **package piecrust mix**	4 **ounces blue cheese**	¼ **cup heavy cream**	⅛ **teaspoon cayenne**	⅛ **teaspoon pepper**
2 **packages (3 ounces each) cream cheese**	2 **tablespoons butter, softened**	3 **eggs**	¼ **teaspoon salt**	1 **teaspoon chopped chives**

1. Prepare piecrust mix following label directions for a single crust. Roll out to a 12-inch round; fit into a 9-inch fluted tart pan with a removable bottom or a 9-inch pie plate.
2. Preheat oven to 375°.
3. Beat cream cheese in a medium-size bowl with electric mixer until softened. Crumble in blue cheese; beat until blended. Add butter, heavy cream, eggs, cayenne, salt and pepper; beat until light and smooth. Stir in chives. Pour into prepared pastry-lined pan.
4. Bake in a preheated moderate oven (375°) for 45 minutes or until tart is puffy and brown. Cool 5 minutes on wire rack. Loosen and remove side of pan. Garnish with additional chopped chives and serve in wedges with fresh fruits, if you wish.

CAPE COD BAKED HAM

A rosy cranberry glaze adds an extra delicious flavor to this popular meat.
Bake at 325° for 1 hour and 30 minutes.
Makes 6 servings plus leftovers.

½ **fully-cooked smoked ham (about 5 pounds)**	1 **can (8 ounces) jellied cranberry sauce**	2 **tablespoons thawed frozen orange juice concentrate**	¼ **cup firmly packed light brown sugar**	1 **tablespoon vinegar** **Pinch ground cloves**

1. Bake ham on rack in roasting pan in a slow oven (325°) for 30 minutes. Remove excess fat and any rind with a sharp knife, leaving a ¼-inch fat layer. Score fat in a diamond pattern.
2. Combine cranberry sauce, orange juice, brown sugar, vinegar and cloves in a small saucepan. Bring to boiling; lower heat; simmer, stirring constantly, 2 minutes. Brush ham with glaze and return to oven.
3. Continue baking ham for 1 hour, brushing with glaze every 15 minutes until all glaze has been used and ham is nicely glazed. Garnish with spinach leaves, if you wish.

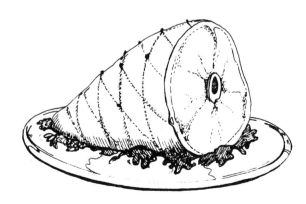

Fourth of July Family Reunion: Iowa Blue Cheese Tart, page 46

HOT AND HEARTY
TEXAS SPARERIBS

Prebaking these ribs assures their juicy tenderness, then they are grilled.
Bake at 450° for 30 minutes; broil or grill for 20 minutes.
Makes 6 servings.

5 pounds country-style spareribs	1 medium-size onion, finely chopped (½ cup) 1 clove garlic, minced	2 tablespoons butter or margarine 1 bottle (12 ounces) chili sauce	¼ cup lemon juice ¼ cup firmly packed light brown sugar	1 teaspoon prepared horseradish 1 teaspoon salt

1. Preheat oven to 450°. Cut ribs into serving-size portions. Place in a shallow baking pan in a single layer.
2. Bake in a preheated very hot oven (450°) for 30 minutes, turning once. Drain off fat.
3. Sauté onion and garlic in butter in a medium-size saucepan until tender, about 3 minutes.

Add chili sauce, lemon juice, sugar, horseradish and salt. Bring to boiling; lower heat; simmer 15 minutes, stirring occasionally.

4. Brush spareribs with sauce. Grill over grayed coals or broil 6 to 7 inches from heat for 20 minutes, brushing with sauce and turning several times until ribs are nicely glazed.

BIG SUR VEGETABLE SALAD
WITH AVOCADO DRESSING

Makes 6 servings.

1½ very ripe avocados, peeled and pitted 1 medium-size onion, sliced ⅔ cup milk 2 tablespoons olive oil 1 teaspoon curry powder 1 teaspoon lemon juice	1 package (9 ounces) frozen cut green beans, blanched and chilled 1 package (4 ounces) alfalfa sprouts 1 can (15 ounces) artichoke hearts 1 large cucumber, sliced	¼ teaspoon salt 1 head red or green leaf lettuce, washed and chilled 1 package (10 ounces) frozen peas, blanched and chilled

1. To make dressing: Combine avocado, onion, milk, olive oil, curry powder, lemon juice and salt in the container of an electric blender; cover; whirl until smooth. Pour into medium-size serving bowl; cover with plastic wrap. Refrigerate until serving time.
2. Line salad bowl with lettuce; arrange peas, green beans, alfalfa sprouts, artichoke hearts and cucumber over greens. Serve with avocado dressing.

CUCUMBER
RELISH

Makes about 18 half pints.

4 quarts diced pared cucumbers (about 8 large cucumbers) 6 large onions, chopped (6 cups)	1 sweet green pepper, halved, seeded and chopped	3 cloves garlic, minced ⅓ cup salt Ice cubes	1½ teaspoons turmeric 5 cups sugar 3 cups vinegar	2 tablespoons prepared mustard 1½ teaspoons celery seeds

1. Combine cucumbers, onions, pepper, garlic and salt in a very large bowl; mix well. Add 6 trays of ice cubes. Refrigerate 2 hours; drain.
2. Combine turmeric, sugar, vinegar, mustard and celery seeds in a large kettle or Dutch oven; mix well. Add drained vegetables. Heat just to boiling.

3. Fill 18 clean hot 8-ounce canning jars to within ¼-inch of top. Seal.
4. Process for 20 minutes in boiling water bath. Cool on wire racks; check seals. Label. Store in a cool, dry place.

GREAT LAKES GARDEN SALAD MOLD

Makes about 6 servings.

1 **package (3 ounces) lemon-flavored gelatin** 1 **envelope unflavored gelatin** 1 **teaspoon salt** 1 **cup boiling water** 2 **cups cold water** ⅓ **cup vinegar** ½ **cup chopped green pepper**	1 **cup shredded carrot** 1 **can (8 ounces) crushed pineapple, drained**	2 **cups shredded green cabbage** **Lettuce**

1. Combine flavored gelatin, unflavored gelatin and salt in a medium-size bowl. Add boiling water, stirring, until gelatin is dissolved.
2. Add cold water and vinegar; refrigerate until thickened to the consistency of unbeaten egg whites.
3. Divide gelatin mixture evenly among 3 medium-size bowls. Add green pepper to one, carrot and pineapple to the second and cabbage to the third.
4. Pour pepper mixture into mold. Put in freezer 10 minutes until sticky-firm. Spoon in carrot mixture; freeze until sticky-firm. Spoon in cabbage mixture. Refrigerate until firm, about 4 hours.
5. Unmold; garnish with lettuce. Serve with mayonnaise or bottled dressing, if you wish.

MEXICAN CORN STICKS

Bake at 400° for 7 minutes.
Makes 21 sticks.

½ **teaspoon salt**
3 **canned jalapeño peppers, chopped**

)0°. Grease 3 corn stick
shortening; put in oven
is heating. (If you have
grease and refill until all
d.)

2. Beat eggs slightly in a large bowl. Add cornmeal, corn, cheese, oil, buttermilk, baking soda and salt; beat until blended. Stir in peppers. Spoon into prepared pans* until almost full.
3. Bake in a preheated hot oven (400°) for about 7 minutes or until firm and golden brown. Remove pans from oven; invert over wire rack; tap sharply. Sticks will drop out. Serve warm.

Batter may be baked in a greased 8×8×2-inch pan for 20 minutes. Cut in squares to serve.

)0°. Grease two 9×1½-
line bottoms with wax
r.
ar, baking powder, salt,
f the milk and the vanilla
at low speed with electric
then at high speed for 2
ining milk and the egg
es longer. Pour into pre-

oven (350°) for 30 min-
Cool on wire rack 10
el off paper; cool.
imore Filling; frost with

Lady Baltimore Frosting. Decorate with additional candied fruits and nuts, if you wish.

Lady Baltimore Filling: Stir 2 tablespoons grated orange rind, ½ cup chopped pecans, ⅓ cup chopped dried figs, ⅓ cup raisins and 4 chopped maraschino cherries into 1½ cups of the frosting.

Lady Baltimore Frosting: Combine 1 cup sugar, ⅓ cup light corn syrup, ¼ cup water and ¼ teaspoon salt in a small saucepan. Cook to 242°. Beat 4 egg whites with ⅛ teaspoon cream of tartar in a large bowl until stiff peaks form. Pour hot syrup into whites in a thin stream, beating until frosting is stiff.

EVERYBODY BRINGS A DISH

Avocado and Bacon Dip*
Ginger-Almond Cheese Spread*
Double-Dipped Fried Chicken*
Barbecued Round Steak*
Creamy Potato Salad*
Macaroni Salad Deluxe*
Corn Relish
Buttermilk Biscuits
Fudgy Chocolate-Orange Cake*
Cherry Pie
Vanilla Ice Cream*
Lemonade   Iced Tea

*Recipe given

AVOCADO AND BACON DIP

The mayonnaise in this creamy dip prevents it from discoloring, so it can be prepared ahead of time and leftovers will keep several days tightly covered in the refrigerator.
Makes 2 cups.

- 2 ripe avocados
- ½ cup mayonnaise
- ¼ cup sliced green onions
- 4 teaspoons lemon juice
- ¾ teaspoon salt
- ¼ teaspoon pepper
- 8 bacon slices, cooked and crumbled

1. Halve avocados; pit, peel and cut in chunks into the container of an electric blender. Add mayonnaise and green onions; cover and whirl to a fairly lumpy puree. Add lemon juice, salt and pepper; whirl again until smooth. Cover and refrigerate until serving time.
2. Just before serving, stir all but 2 tablespoons of the bacon into the dip and spoon into a serving bowl. Sprinkle dip with reserved bacon.

GINGER-ALMOND CHEESE SPREAD

The piquant sweetness of ginger is combined with the crunch of toasted almonds.
Makes 3 cups.

- 2 packages (8 ounces each) cream cheese, softened
- 1 jar (10 ounces) preserved ginger, drained and finely chopped
- 2 teaspoons lemon juice
- 1 cup blanched almonds, toasted and chopped

1. Combine cheese and all but 2 tablespoons of the ginger, lemon juice and ¾ cup of the almonds in a medium-size bowl; blend well.
2. Line a 3-cup bowl with plastic wrap. Spoon cheese mixture into bowl, packing it down firmly; refrigerate.
3. To serve: Turn cheese ball out onto serving platter. Peel off plastic wrap. Garnish with reserved ginger and almonds.

DOUBLE-DIPPED FRIED CHICKEN

Tender and moist, with a crunchy crust.
Makes 8 servings.

2 broiler-fryers (about 3 pounds each), cut up
1 cup light cream or half-and-half
2 cups all-purpose flour
3½ teaspoons salt
½ teaspoon pepper
1 teaspoon paprika
1 teaspoon poultry seasoning
Vegetable oil or shortening for frying

1. Place chicken pieces in a large, shallow dish; pour cream over top; turn chicken to coat. Cover; refrigerate several hours.
2. Combine flour, salt, pepper, paprika and poultry seasoning in a plastic bag. Add chicken pieces, a few at a time, and shake to coat well. Dip each again in remaining cream; shake again in the flour mixture.
3. Pour enough oil or melt enough shortening in a large, heavy saucepan or Dutch oven to make a depth of 2 inches; heat to 350° on a deep-fat frying thermometer.
4. Fry chicken pieces, a few at a time, turning once. Fry breast, leg and thighs about 18 to 20 minutes and wings about 12 minutes or until crisp and tender. Remove to paper toweling to drain. Serve at room temperature or refrigerate to serve cold. Arrange chicken in a basket. Garnish with carrot curls, radish roses and parsley, if you wish.

BARBECUED ROUND STEAK

The zippy marinade tenderizes as well as adds great flavor.
Makes 8 servings.

½ cup vegetable oil
¼ cup red wine vinegar
2 tablespoons Worcestershire sauce
3 cloves garlic, minced
1 beef round steak (about 2½ pounds), cut 1½ inches thick

1. Combine oil, vinegar, Worcestershire and garlic in a shallow glass dish just large enough to hold meat.
2. Pierce meat in several places with fork; add to marinade; turn to coat. Cover with plastic wrap. Refrigerate several hours, preferably overnight, turning several times. Remove from refrigerator 1 hour before cooking.
3. Place on charcoal grill 6 inches from greyed coals or on rack of broiler pan. Broil 6 inches from heat. Cook to desired doneness, brushing occasionally with marinade and turning once. For rare, cook 8 to 12 minutes each side; medium, 12 to 15 minutes; well, 15 to 20 minutes.

CREAMY POTATO SALAD

Marinate the warm potatoes in oil and vinegar for deep-down flavor.
Makes 12 servings.

7 to 8 medium-size potatoes (4 pounds)
¼ cup vegetable oil
¼ cup cider vinegar
1 tablespoon salt
½ teaspoon pepper
1 large onion, finely chopped (1 cup)

1 medium-size green pepper, seeded and diced (1 cup)
½ cup mayonnaise or salad dressing

1 cup diagonally sliced celery
½ cup dairy sour cream
Leaf lettuce
Tomato wedges

1. Cook potatoes in boiling water to cover in a large saucepan until tender, about 30 minutes. Drain, peel and cut in large cubes into a large bowl.
2. Add oil, vinegar, salt, pepper and onion. Toss just until potatoes are moistened. Cover; refrigerate 2 to 3 hours or until marinade is absorbed.
3. Add green pepper and celery to potatoes; combine mayonnaise and sour cream; toss gently to coat with dressing. Chill until serving time. To serve: Line salad bowl with lettuce, mound potato salad in center; arrange tomato wedges around edge.

Overleaf: Everybody Brings a Dish: Macaroni Salad Deluxe, page 54; Double-Dipped Fried Chicken, page 51; Creamy Potato Salad, page 51

MACARONI SALAD DELUXE

Makes 12 servings.

1 package (1 pound) small shell macaroni	2 teaspoons grated lemon rind	6 ounces Swiss cheese, cut into small cubes (1½ cups)
1 cup mayonnaise or salad dressing	2 tablespoons lemon juice	1 cup thinly sliced green onions (about 1 bunch) Chicory
1 container (8 ounces) plain yogurt	1 teaspoon salt ½ teaspoon pepper	
¾ cup milk	1 package (10 ounces) frozen peas, thawed	

1. Cook macaroni following label directions; drain.
2. Mix mayonnaise, yogurt, milk, lemon rind, lemon juice, salt and pepper in a large bowl until smooth.
3. Add macaroni, peas, Swiss cheese and green onions to mixture. Toss gently to coat with dressing. Refrigerate salad until serving time.
4. To serve: Line salad bowl with chicory; mound macaroni salad in center.

FUDGY CHOCOLATE ORANGE CAKE

Bake at 350° for 45 minutes.
Makes 12 servings.

3 squares unsweetened chocolate	1 tablespoon grated orange rind	1 cup boiling water Chocolate Orange Frosting *(recipe follows)*
2¼ cups *sifted* cake flour	1½ teaspoons vanilla	
2 teaspoons baking soda	1 container (8 ounces) dairy sour cream	
½ teaspoon salt		
½ cup (1 stick) butter or margarine		
2¼ cups firmly packed light brown sugar		
3 eggs		

1. Melt chocolate in a small bowl over hot, not boiling, water; cool.
2. Sift flour, baking soda and salt onto wax paper. Preheat oven to 350°.
3. Beat butter in large bowl with electric mixer until soft. Add brown sugar and eggs; beat at high speed until light and fluffy, about 5 minutes. Beat in orange rind, vanilla and cooled chocolate.
4. Add dry ingredients alternately with sour cream, beating at low speed of electric mixer until batter is smooth. Stir in boiling water. (The batter will be thin.)
5. Pour into a greased and floured 13 × 9 × 2-inch baking pan.
6. Bake in preheated moderate oven (350°) for 45 minutes or until center springs back when lightly pressed with fingertip. Cool completely in pan on wire rack. Frost with Chocolate Orange Frosting. Garnish with orange slices and walnuts, if you wish.

Chocolate Orange Frosting: Melt 2 squares unsweetened chocolate and ¼ cup (½ stick) butter or margarine in a medium-size bowl over hot, not boiling, water; cool. Beat in 2 cups 10X (confectioners') sugar alternately with ¼ cup orange juice and 1 teaspoon vanilla until smooth and spreadable.

VANILLA ICE CREAM

Makes 2 quarts.

1½ cups sugar	4 eggs, slightly beaten	1 quart (4 cups), heavy cream
¼ cup all-purpose flour		
¼ teaspoon salt		
2 cups milk		
1 two-inch piece vanilla bean OR: 2 tablespoons vanilla		

1. Combine sugar, flour, salt and milk in a large saucepan.
2. If using vanilla bean, cut in half lengthwise and scrape out the tiny seeds. Add seeds and pod to milk mixture in saucepan.
3. Cook, stirring constantly, over medium heat, until mixture thickens and bubbles 2 minutes.
4. Stir half the hot mixture slowly into beaten eggs in a medium-size bowl; stir mixture back into remaining mixture in pan. Cook, stirring constantly, 1 minute. Pour into a large bowl; stir in cream and vanilla (if vanilla bean not used). Chill at least 2 hours. If vanilla bean is used, remove pod from mixture before pouring into a 4- to 6-quart freezer can; freeze, following manufacturer's directions.
5. Serve soft-frozen or pack in plastic container; freeze until firm.

Labor Day Cookout: Herb-Grilled Chicken, page 57; Beef and Vegetable Kabobs, page 57

ON LABOR DAY

HAVE A COOKOUT FOR
THE LAST BASH OF SUMMER.

Observed on the first Monday in September, Labor Day was first celebrated with a parade in New York City in 1882. It's the day we honor all who work. Originally, Labor Day was the culmination of the Labor movement. After the Industrial Revolution in the 18th century, a working class emerged. As more and more people worked in factories together, they organized to rally for better wages and working conditions. To acknowledge the contributions that labor has made to America, a major union decided to set aside a day for a holiday. Since then, individual state laws in the late 1800's and early 1900's have legalized the observance as a holiday. Today, Labor Day is celebrated with picnics and cookouts. Labor Day comes midway between the Fourth of July and Thanksgiving. It's

---

LABOR DAY COOKOUT

Creamy Shrimp Dip*
with Carrot, Celery and Cucumber Sticks
Barbecued Sirloin Steak
Herb-Grilled Chicken*
Beef and Vegetable Kabobs*
Foil-Baked Potatoes
Summer Squash with Bacon and Onion
Stuffing*
Corn on the Cob
Garlic Bread
Chocolate Cream Cake*
Watermelon Basket of Fruit
Beer   Soft Drinks

*Recipe given

---

the last celebration of summer, marking vacation's end for school children and the start of the fall season. It's a time for taking to the roads for the last bash of summer. Celebrate Labor Day with a fun-filled barbecue. Our menu teams the heartiness of grilled chicken and kabobs with steak. It's the perfect party for warm-weather entertaining. Foods taste so much better when they're hot off the grill. The accompaniments, such as baked potatoes, squash, corn on the cob and bread, can all be prepared on the grill. A watermelon carved into a basket, then filled with fresh summer fruit, plus old-fashioned chocolate cake are perfect endings for a perfect day. Everyone will want to sink their teeth into these fun-filled party foods, and return for seconds!

CREAMY SHRIMP DIP

A small quantity of tiny shrimp in a rich, delicately seasoned creamy sauce makes this luxurious shrimp-cocktail-in-a-dip. Makes 2⅓ cups.

1 cup mayonnaise ½ cup dairy sour cream 2 tablespoons catsup 2 tablespoons minced onion	1 tablespoon dry sherry *(optional)* ½ teaspoon Worcestershire sauce ⅛ teaspoon cayenne	1 package (6 ounces) frozen cooked tiny shrimp, thawed according to package directions and drained

1. Blend mayonnaise, sour cream, catsup, onion, sherry, Worcestershire and cayenne in a medium-size bowl. Add shrimp and mix well.
2. Spoon into a serving bowl and serve at once, or cover and refrigerate up to 5 hours before serving.

HERB-GRILLED CHICKEN

The sauce is best made a few hours in advance of using. If refrigerated, whip it for a few seconds. It can be used on chicken parts or on a whole spit-roasted chicken.
Makes 8 servings.

½ cup vegetable oil ¼ cup cider vinegar 1 egg 1 tablespoon salt ¼ teaspoon pepper 1 teaspoon poultry seasoning	¼ teaspoon leaf oregano, crumbled ⅛ teaspoon leaf thyme, crumbled Pinch garlic powder	Pinch paprika 2 broiler-fryers (about 2½ pounds each), quartered

1. Combine oil, vinegar, egg, salt, pepper, poultry seasoning, oregano, thyme, garlic powder and paprika in a small bowl; beat with a fork to blend. Brush over chicken.
2. Grill chicken, skin-side up, 6 inches from hot coals, 15 minutes. Turn and baste with sauce. Continue turning and basting about 30 minutes longer or until chicken is tender but not dry.

BEEF AND VEGETABLE KABOBS

Grill 12 to 15 minutes.
Makes 4 servings.

1 chuck steak, 1½ inches thick (about 2 pounds) ½ pint cherry tomatoes ½ pound mushrooms 2 green peppers 1 jar (16 ounces) whole onions in liquid 1 jar (6 ounces) marinated artichoke hearts ½ cup vegetable oil ¼ cup honey	2 tablespoons vinegar 2 tablespoons soy sauce 1 large clove garlic, minced 2 tablespoons minced parsley	1 teaspoon ground ginger 1 teaspoon coarse salt ½ teaspoon cracked pepper

1. Cut steak into 1½-inch cubes. Prepare vegetables, leaving tomatoes and mushroom caps whole if small; seed peppers and cut into squares; drain onions and artichoke hearts, reserving liquids.
2. Combine oil, honey, vinegar, soy sauce, garlic, parsley, ginger, salt and pepper with reserved liquids. Pour marinade mixture into a large, shallow nonmetal dish. Add meat cubes.
3. Let marinate for 1 to 24 hours, turning occasionally. Cover dish and refrigerate.
4. Thread vegetables, except peppers, on skewers and brush generously with marinade. Remove meat from marinade. Pat with paper toweling to remove excess marinade. Thread meat and peppers alternately on other skewers.
5. Grill meat 5 inches from hot coals 12 to 15 minutes for rare, turning skewers several times and basting with the marinade. Grill vegetables about 5 to 8 minutes, brushing with marinade and turning several times until tender.

SUMMER SQUASH WITH BACON AND ONION STUFFING

Zucchini can be used in place of yellow summer squash in this side dish.
Makes 8 servings.

4 medium-size yellow summer squash (⅔ pound each) **½ teaspoon salt**	**8 bacon slices, cut crosswise into ¼-inch pieces** **⅔ cup chopped onion** **⅔ cup chopped fresh parsley**	**2 tablespoons packaged bread crumbs** **1 teaspoon leaf basil, crumbled** **½ teaspoon salt**

1. Cut squash in half lengthwise. Scoop out inside pulp, using a spoon, leaving a ¼-inch-thick shell. Chop pulp coarsely; sprinkle shells with ½ teaspoon salt.
2. Cook bacon in a large skillet until crisp; drain, crumble, reserve. Add onion and chopped squash to bacon drippings in skillet; sauté 2 minutes, stirring frequently until just tender. Remove from heat and stir in parsley, bread crumbs, basil, ½ teaspoon salt and reserved bacon. Spoon into squash shells and place in an aluminum-foil baking pan; cover with foil.
3. Place pan on grill; cook squash for 25 minutes or until tender. Place squash directly on grill to brown slightly.

CHOCOLATE CREAM CAKE

Bake at 350° for 35 minutes.
Makes 12 servings.

3 squares unsweetened chocolate **2¼ cups *sifted* cake flour** **2 teaspoons baking soda** **½ teaspoon salt** **½ cup (1 stick) butter or margarine, softened** **2¼ cups firmly packed light brown sugar**	**3 eggs** **1½ teaspoons vanilla** **1 container (8 ounces) dairy sour cream**	**1 cup boiling water** **Whipped Cocoa Cream *(recipe follows)***

1. Melt chocolate in a small bowl over hot, not boiling, water; cool.
2. Grease and flour two 9 × 1½-inch cake pans; tap out excess flour.
3. Sift flour, baking soda and salt onto wax paper. Preheat oven to 350°.
4. Beat butter, sugar and eggs in a large bowl with electric mixer on high speed, until light and fluffy. Beat in vanilla and chocolate.

5. Stir in dry ingredients, alternating with sour cream, beating well with a spoon until smooth. Stir in water. (Batter will be thin.) Pour into prepared pans.
6. Bake in a preheated moderate oven (350°) for 35 minutes or until centers spring back when lightly pressed with fingertip. Cool in pans 10 minutes; turn out on wire racks; cool completely. Split each layer in half crosswise to make 4 thin layers.
7. Fill and frost with Whipped Cocoa Cream. Refrigerate.

Whipped Cocoa Cream: Whip 1 pint heavy cream, ⅔ cup 10X (confectioners') sugar, ½ cup unsweetened cocoa powder and 1 teaspoon vanilla in a medium-size bowl until stiff.

HALLOWEEN

THERE'S NO TRICK
BUT LOTS OF TREATS HERE.

What began as a religious and New Year's celebration is now a children's day of fun and frollicking. Many of the Halloween symbols originated with the ancient Celts of Ireland and Great Britain. Halloween was All Hallows E'en, the evening before All Hallows or Saints' Day, November 1, which was New Year's Day for the Celts. In addition, that day honored their Sun God and the Lord of the Dead, Samhain. The Halloween bonfire ritual can be traced to the Druids (priests of the Celts) who set fire to animal and human sacrifices. The Romans, who later conquered the Druids, prohibited such sacrifices. In Europe during the Middle Ages, black cats were thrown into fires because they were believed to be transformed witches. Later, the Christians no longer offered such sacrifices but killed animals for food in the name of God. In later times, the fire was thought to keep away evil spirits such as ghosts and witches. The custom of trick or treating goes back to the pagan days. Ghosts were thought to be around the houses of the living. They were treated to a feast by masked, costumed villagers representing the souls of the dead. The villagers tricked the ghosts and led them away. With Christianity, costumed children paraded around on the eve of All

---

JACK O'LANTERN PARTY FOR KIDS

Apples for Bobbing
Cheese Snacks*
Frankfurters
Toasted Buns
Pickles, Olives, Chips
Carrot-Walnut Cupcakes*
Frozen Bananas on a Stick*

*Recipe given

Souls' Day, the day after All Saints' Day, offering to fast for the souls of the dead in exchange for money or gifts. In America, Halloween is divorced from any religious significance. To children of all ages, it's a day of partying, and our menus can help liven things up.

Bobbing for apples and carving a jack o'lantern are old Irish customs. But instead of a pumpkin, Irish children hollowed out large turnips or potatoes and inserted a candle inside. How the jack o'lantern got its name is an old tale. Supposedly, an Irishman named Jack tricked the Devil and made the Devil swear not to take his soul. When Jack died, he was turned away from heaven. The Devil wouldn't take him either but threw him a hot coal from the fires of Hell and told him to go back to where he came from. Jack was eating a turnip at the time and put the coal inside. Since then, Jack has used the light searching for his final place of rest. To this day, the jack o'lantern is used to light porches, fence posts and windows for welcoming trick or treaters on Halloween night. In planning a party for children, have plenty of activities and games. Let them make a goodie bag from brown paper bags to carry their treats home.

CHEESE SNACKS

This dough can be prepared ahead and refrigerated until ready to use.
Bake at 350° for 15 minutes.
Makes about 6 servings.

¼ cup vegetable oil 1 cup whole wheat flour	4 ounces sharp Cheddar cheese, shredded (1 cup)	½ teaspoon salt ¼ teaspoon leaf sage, crumbled	¼ teaspoon leaf thyme, crumbled	Pinch cayenne 2 to 3 tablespoons cold water

1. Combine oil, flour, cheese, salt, sage, thyme and cayenne in a medium-size bowl. Add water gradually to make a dough. Cover; refrigerate until firm, about 15 minutes.
2. Preheat oven to 350°. Roll dough on lightly floured surface to make a 12-inch circle. Cut with 1½-inch round or scalloped cookie cutter. Place on ungreased cookie sheets ½ inch apart. Prick each cracker with a fork. Reroll dough to use scraps.
3. Bake in a preheated moderate oven (350°) for 15 minutes. Remove to wire rack to cool. Store in tightly covered container.

CARROT-WALNUT CUPCAKES

These moist and spicy cupcakes are delicious plain or frosted.
Bake at 350° for 20 minutes.
Makes 18 cupcakes.

1½ cups whole wheat flour 1½ teaspoons baking soda ½ teaspoon salt	1 teaspoon ground cinnamon ½ teaspoon ground nutmeg	1 cup vegetable oil ½ cup honey 2 eggs 1 teaspoon vanilla	2 to 3 medium-size carrots, finely shredded (1½ cups)	1 cup finely chopped walnuts Honey Cream Cheese Frosting *(recipe follows)* ½ cup chopped walnuts

1. Line 18 medium-size muffin-pan cups with paper baking cups or grease the cups. Preheat oven to 350°.
2. Sift flour, baking soda, salt, cinnamon and nutmeg onto wax paper.
3. Combine oil, honey, eggs and vanilla in a large bowl; beat until creamy and thick. Stir in flour mixture until batter is smooth. Add carrots and walnuts; mix well. Spoon batter into prepared pans, filling half full.
4. Bake in a preheated moderate oven (350°) for 20 minutes or until tops spring back when lightly pressed with fingertip. Cool cupcakes in pan on wire rack about 5 minutes; remove cupcakes from pans. Cool completely. Frost with Honey Cream Cheese Frosting; sprinkle with chopped nuts.

Honey Cream Cheese Frosting: Whip 1 package (8 ounces) cream cheese, softened, with 2 tablespoons honey in a medium-size bowl.

FROZEN BANANAS ON A STICK

Makes 10 snacks.

5 firm ripe bananas, each 8 inches long 1 package (12 ounces) peanut butter chips 2 teaspoons vegetable shortening 2 squares unsweetened chocolate

1. Cut 5 bananas in half crosswise; push a flat wooden skewer halfway into center of cut edge. Melt peanut butter chips with shortening in a medium-size bowl over simmering water. Peel banana halves. Hold banana by skewer over melted chips and coat evenly with melted peanut butter chips, using a small metal spatula. Place coated bananas on a chilled cookie sheet.
2. Melt unsweetened chocolate in a small bowl over simmering water in a small saucepan. Drizzle chocolate over each coated banana, using a small spoon. Place cookie sheet in freezer. When bananas are firm, wrap individually in plastic wrap or aluminum foil. Eat while still frozen.

> **ORANGE AND BLACK TIE PARTY**
>
> *Harvest Pumpkin Soup*
> *Marinated Sirloin Tip**
> *Vegetable Platter**
> *with Fluffy Hollandaise Sauce**
> *Iceberg Lettuce with Green Goddess Dressing**
> *Dinner Rolls*
> *Chocolate Cheese Torte**
> *Brandied Cider**
>
> **Recipe given*

HARVEST PUMPKIN SOUP

Makes 8 servings.

- 1 **large onion, sliced (1 cup)**
- 2 **tablespoons butter or margarine**
- 2 **cans condensed chicken broth**
- 1 **can (16 ounces) pumpkin**
- 1 **teaspoon salt**
- ¾ **teaspoon ground cinnamon**
- ¼ **teaspoon ground nutmeg**
- ⅛ **teaspoon pepper**
- 1 **cup light cream or half-and-half**

Cinamon-Sugar Toast Triangles (recipe follows)

1. Sauté onion in butter in a large saucepan until soft, about 5 minutes. Add 1 can of the chicken broth; bring to boiling; cover; lower heat; simmer 10 minutes.
2. Place ½ cup of the onion mixture in container of electric blender; cover. Whirl until smooth. Add remaining onion broth mixture and whirl until smooth. Return to saucepan.
3. Add remaining can of chicken broth, pumpkin, salt, cinnamon, nutmeg and pepper. Stir until smooth. Bring to boiling; cover. Lower heat; simmer 10 minutes.
4. Slowly stir in cream; heat just until thoroughly hot. Serve with Cinnamon-Sugar Toast Triangles, if you wish.

Cinnamon-Sugar Toast Triangles: Blend 3 tablespoons softened butter or margarine with 1 tablespoon sugar and ½ teaspoon ground cinnamon in a small bowl. Spread generously on 4 slices of cracked wheat or whole wheat bread. Place on a cookie sheet. Bake in a preheated hot oven (400°) for 8 minutes or until bubbly and golden brown. Cut each bread slice into 4 triangles. Makes 16 triangles.

MARINATED SIRLOIN TIP

Roast at 325° for 1 hour and 10 minutes.
Makes 8 servings.

- 1 **sirloin tip roast (3½ pounds)**
- 1½ **cups vegetable oil**
- ½ **cup red wine vinegar**
- 1 **jar (3 ounces) capers, drained**
- 2 **cloves garlic, minced**
- 2 **tablespoons snipped chives**
- 1½ **teaspoons sugar**
- 1½ **teaspoons dry mustard**
- 1½ **teaspoons leaf oregano, crumbled**
- 1½ **teaspoons pepper**
- ¼ **teaspoon liquid hot pepper seasoning**
- 3 **bunches watercress**
- 2 **pints cherry tomatoes, halved**
- 2 **red onions, quartered lengthwise and slivered**

1. Wipe roast with damp paper toweling. Place, fat-side up, on rack in an open roasting pan. Insert meat thermometer into the center of the meat.
2. Roast in a slow oven (325°), allowing 20 to 25 minutes per pound or about 1 hour and 10 minutes for rare (140°); 30 to 35 minutes per pound or about 1 hour and 45 minutes for medium (160°). Remove from oven; cool to room temperature.
3. While roast is cooling, combine oil, vinegar, capers, garlic, chives, sugar, dry mustard, oregano, pepper and hot pepper seasoning in a large jar with a screw-top. Cover jar securely; shake to blend well.
4. Slice roast very thinly with a sharp knife or electric carving knife. Place in a large shallow dish; shake marinade and pour ½ of the marinade over meat. Cover with plastic wrap; refrigerate overnight.
5. To serve: Arrange watercress around edges of large serving platter; lift meat slices out of marinade and overlap in rows on platter, then arrange cherry tomatoes and red onion slivers; place small bunch of watercress in center of the platter; spoon any marinade in pan over meat slices. Pour marinade in jar into small serving bowl. Let each guest spoon additional marinade over meat and vegetables.

VEGETABLE PLATTER

Makes 8 servings.

1 bunch (2 pounds) broccoli
2 bunches (1 pound each) carrots
Fluffy Hollandaise Sauce (recipe follows)

1. Trim and discard outer leaves and tough ends from broccoli. Split large stalks lengthwise. Cook in boiling salted water about 10 minutes or until tender. Drain; keep warm.
2. Pare carrots; cut into thin sticks. Cook in boiling salted water about 20 minutes or until tender. Drain; keep warm.
3. Prepare Fluffy Hollandaise Sauce. Arrange vegetables on warm serving platter. Spoon sauce over.

FLUFFY HOLLANDAISE SAUCE

A fluffy version of the classic sauce.
Makes 1⅔ cups.

½ cup (1 stick) butter or margarine
¼ cup hot water
4 egg yolks
2 tablespoons lemon juice
¼ teaspoon salt
Dash cayenne

1. Melt butter in top of a double boiler over simmering water; stir in hot water. Remove top from heat and set on work surface.
2. Add unbeaten egg yolks all at once; beat with electric mixer or rotary beater 2 to 3 minutes or until mixture is almost double in bulk. Stir in lemon juice, salt and cayenne.
3. Place over simmering water again; cook, stirring constantly, 5 minutes or until thickened.

(Be sure water in lower part does not touch bottom of upper part or boil at any time during cooking.)
4. Remove sauce from heat; let stand, uncovered, until serving time. To reheat: Place over simmering water again and stir lightly for 2 to 3 minutes. (In reheating, sauce may lose some of its fluffiness but it will keep its golden-rich creaminess.)

ICEBERG LETTUCE WITH GREEN GODDESS DRESSING

Makes 8 servings.

1 teaspoon leaf tarragon, crumbled
¼ cup tarragon vinegar
1 cup mayonnaise or salad dressing
1 container (8 ounces) dairy sour cream
½ cup chopped fresh parsley
2 tablespoons chopped chives
2 tablespoons anchovy paste
1 tablespoon lemon juice
1 clove garlic, minced
1 large head iceberg lettuce

1. Soak tarragon in vinegar 10 minutes; strain vinegar mixture into small bowl; discard tarragon.
2. Blend mayonnaise, sour cream, parsley, chives, anchovy paste, lemon juice and garlic into vinegar; cover; chill at least 1 hour.
3. To serve: Cut lettuce into 8 wedges. Arrange on individual salad plates. Pass dressing to spoon over.

CHOCOLATE CHEESE TORTE

Bake at 350° for 40 minutes.
Makes 12 servings.

1⅓ cups graham cracker crumbs 3 tablespoons sugar 3 tablespoons unsweetened cocoa powder	⅓ cup butter or margarine, melted 4 packages (3 ounces each) cream cheese, softened	¾ cup sugar 2 eggs 2 tablespoons coffee-flavored liqueur or rum 1½ teaspoons vanilla 1 container (8 ounces) dairy sour cream	1 square unsweetened chocolate, grated 1½ teaspoons instant coffee powder 2 tablespoons boiling water	4 squares semi-sweet chocolate 4 eggs, separated ⅓ cup sugar ½ cup heavy cream, whipped

1. Blend crumbs, 3 tablespoons sugar, cocoa and butter together until well mixed. Press firmly onto the bottom and side of a 9-inch springform pan.
2. Bake in a moderate oven (350°) for 10 minutes. Cool while preparing filling.
3. Beat cream cheese in a large bowl with electric mixer at high speed until light and fluffy. Gradually beat in ¾ cup sugar. Add the 2 eggs, 1 at a time, beating well after each addition. Add 1 tablespoon of the liqueur and 1 teaspoon of the vanilla. Turn into baked crust.
4. Bake in a moderate oven (350°) for 30 minutes. Cool for 10 minutes on wire rack.
5. Gently spread sour cream over baked layer. Sprinkle with grated chocolate. Refrigerate.
6. Dissolve coffee in boiling water in the top of a double boiler over hot, not boiling, water. Add chocolate. Stir until melted and blended.
7. Beat the 4 egg yolks in a medium-size bowl with an electric mixer until thick. Gradually beat in ⅓ cup sugar. Add a small amount of chocolate mixture. Beat well. Continue adding small amounts of chocolate mixture to egg mixture, beating until all has been added. Add remaining 1 tablespoon liqueur and ½ teaspoon vanilla.
8. Beat egg whites until stiff. Gently fold into chocolate mixture. Spread over cooled baked layer. Refrigerate until firm. When ready to serve, loosen side of pan; remove. Place cake on serving plate. Decorate with whipped cream.

BRANDIED CIDER

Makes 8 servings.

2 quarts apple cider 1½ teaspoons whole cloves	¾ teaspoon whole allspice 2 three-inch pieces stick cinnamon	1¼ cups California brandy Orange or lemon slices (optional)

1. Combine cider, cloves, allspice and cinnamon in a large saucepan. Bring slowly to boiling; lower heat. Simmer 15 minutes. Remove spices. Add brandy.
2. Pour into punch bowl or individual cups. Add orange or lemon slices to each cup of cider, if you wish.

THANKSGIVING

A TIME TO GIVE THANKS AND FEAST.

The Pilgrims observed America's first Thanksgiving in 1621, but the idea of a harvest festival paying homage to a supreme being for a good season goes back several thousand years. Many thanksgiving celebrations were agricultural and religious in nature. A successful harvest meant food and survival during the cold winter to come. The first Pilgrim Thanksgiving menu was varied and extensive. They had venison, duck, seafood, corn breads, wild fruits and berries in addition to turkey and pumpkin or squash. The observance of this holiday by the Pilgrims was not a regular occurrence. It was President Washington who proclaimed the first national Thanksgiving Day in 1789 to be Thursday, November 26. However, many people regarded it as a strictly religious holiday and many states did not observe it. Thanksgiving Day did not become

---

HARVEST FESTIVAL DINNER

Mushroom Soup Supreme*
Roast Ribs of Beef*
with Whipped Horseradish Cream*
Potato Nests*
with Buttered Pimiento Lima Beans
Marinated Cherry Tomatoes
Cranberry Pecan Muffins*
Popovers*
Praline Pumpkin Pie
with Praline Lace Cones*
Demitasse
Brandy

*Recipe given

---

a national holiday celebrated across the country until President Lincoln's proclamation. Today, it is always celebrated on the fourth Thursday in November. Thanksgiving is traditionally a family day celebrated with a large meal at home. Although certain foods such as turkey, cranberries and pumpkin pie are associated with Thanksgiving, a modern menu can include prime ribs of beef or ham. Here, we have included a traditional Thanksgiving spread with delicious oyster soup to begin the meal, a savory stuffing for the turkey, fabulous vegetables and a sparkling cranberry relish mold. There is a choice of two splendid desserts to finish it all off. The other menu features succulent prime ribs of beef served with a horseradish cream sauce. It's sure to be a feast day the family will remember with these menus.

MUSHROOM SOUP SUPREME

Smooth and creamy with a flavorful chicken broth base.
Makes 8 to 10 servings.

1 **pound small
mushrooms**
¼ **cup (½ stick)
butter or
margarine**
1 **tablespoon
lemon juice**
2 **tablespoons flour**
1 **teaspoon salt**
8 **cups water**
4 **envelopes or
teaspoons
instant chicken
broth**
4 **egg yolks**
1 **tablespoon dry
sherry**

1. Wash mushrooms; trim ends off stems, then cut through caps and stems to make paper-thin slices.
2. Sauté, stirring often, in butter in a kettle, 2 minutes. Sprinkle with lemon juice; toss lightly to mix.
3. Blend in flour and salt; stir in water and instant chicken broth. Cook, stirring constantly, until mixture thickens and bubbles 3 minutes.
4. Beat egg yolks well with sherry in a small bowl; blend in about a half cup of the hot mushroom mixture, then stir back into remaining mixture in saucepan. Heat, stirring constantly, 1 minute.
5. Ladle soup into tureen. Garnish with chopped fresh parsley, if you wish.

ROAST RIBS OF BEEF

Roast at 325° for 1½ to 2 hours.
Makes 8 servings.

1 **beef standing rib
roast (about 4
pounds)
Whipped
Horseradish
Cream** (recipe
follows)

1. Place beef, fat-side up, in shallow roasting pan. If using meat thermometer, insert so bulb is not touching bone or resting in fat. It is not necessary to add water or to baste.
2. Roast in a slow oven (325°) for 20 minutes a pound for rare (140° on meat thermometer), 25 minutes for medium (160°), or 27 to 30 minutes for well-done (170°). Meat should be allowed to stand 30 minutes for easier carving. Since it will continue to cook when removed from oven, it should be removed when thermometer registers about 10° below selected temperature.
3. Carve in slices across the grain, using tip of knife to loosen slices as you carve. Serve with Whipped Horseradish Cream.

Whipped Horseradish Cream: Combine 1 cup heavy cream, 1 tablespoon prepared horseradish, ¼ teaspoon Worcestershire sauce and a dash of liquid hot pepper seasoning in a small bowl. Beat with electric mixer until soft peaks form. Refrigerate. Makes about 2 cups.

POTATO NESTS

Makes 8 servings.

10 **to 12 large
baking potatoes,
pared
Vegetable oil for
frying**

1. Coarsely shred potatoes into a large bowl of cold water. Drain. Pat dry on paper toweling.
2. Fill a large saucepan ⅔ full with vegetable oil; heat to 400° on a deep-fat frying thermometer. Dip bottom of a wire potato basket in hot oil. Press about 1½ cups potatoes into basket, leaving center open.
3. Dip top in oil; press halves together; secure with clip. Lower slowly into oil; fry 4 to 5 minutes or until golden brown. Remove nest from basket to paper toweling; keep warm. Repeat. Fill potato nests with buttered lima beans, if you wish. Can be reheated in a moderate oven (375°).

CRANBERRY PECAN MUFFINS

Bake at 400° for 20 minutes.
Makes 2½ dozen muffins.

1½ cups coarsely chopped cranberries
¼ cup sugar
3 cups *sifted* all-purpose flour
4½ teaspoons baking powder
½ teaspoon salt
1 cup sugar

½ cup vegetable shortening
1 cup chopped pecans

2 teaspoons grated lemon rind
2 eggs
1 cup milk

1. Preheat oven to 400°. Combine cranberries and ¼ cup sugar in a small bowl; let stand while preparing batter.
2. Sift flour, baking powder, salt and 1 cup sugar into a large bowl. Cut in shortening with a pastry blender until mixture is crumbly. Stir in pecans and lemon rind.
3. Beat eggs in a small bowl until light; stir in milk. Add liquid all at once to flour mixture, stirring just until moist. Fold in cranberry mixture. Spoon batter into greased medium-size muffin-pan cups, filling each ⅔ full.
4. Bake in a preheated hot oven (400°) for 20 minutes or until golden brown. Remove from pans to wire racks. Serve warm with butter and honey.

POPOVERS

Bake at 425° for 40 minutes.
Makes 8 popovers.

2 eggs
1 cup milk
1 tablespoon butter or margarine, melted
1 cup *sifted* all-purpose flour
½ teaspoon salt

1. Preheat oven to 425°. Generously butter eight 5-ounce custard cups; place on jelly-roll pan.
2. Beat eggs in a medium-size bowl until frothy. Stir in milk and melted butter; beat until blended. Beat in flour and salt until batter is smooth. Ladle into prepared cups, filling each about half full.
3. Bake in a preheated hot oven (425°) for 35 minutes. Cut slit in side of each popover to allow steam to escape. Return to oven and bake 5 minutes longer or until popovers are deep brown and very crisp. Serve with butter and jelly.

PRALINE PUMPKIN PIE

A thin layer of crunchy praline bakes under the creamy pumpkin custard.
Bake at 450° for 10 minutes, then at 350° for 50 minutes.
Makes one 9-inch pie.

½ package piecrust mix
3 tablespoons butter or margarine

⅓ cup firmly packed brown sugar
⅓ cup chopped pecans
1 cup evaporated milk

½ cup water
3 eggs
1½ cups (from a 1-pound can) pumpkin
½ cup granulated sugar

½ cup firmly packed brown sugar
1½ teaspoons pumpkin pie spice

1 teaspoon salt
½ cup heavy cream, whipped
Praline Lace Cones *(recipe follows)*

1. Preheat oven to 450°. Prepare piecrust mix following label directions. Roll out to a 12-inch round on lightly floured pastry board; fit into a 9-inch pie plate; trim overhang to ½ inch; turn under, flush with rim; flute to make a stand-up edge.
2. Cream butter with the ⅓ cup brown sugar in small bowl; stir in pecans. Press over bottom of prepared shell in an even layer.
3. Bake in a preheated very hot oven (450°) for 10 minutes; remove; cool on wire rack 10 minutes. Lower heat to moderate (350°).
4. Combine milk and water in a 2-cup measure. Beat eggs slightly in large bowl; stir in pumpkin, granulated sugar, the ½ cup brown sugar, pumpkin pie spice and salt; beat in milk mixture. Pour into cooled pastry shell.
5. Bake in a preheated moderate oven (350°) for 50 minutes or until center is set but still soft. (Do not overbake—custard will set as it cools.) Cool completely on wire rack.
6. Top with a crown of whipped cream; decorate with Praline Lace Cones.

Harvest Festival Dinner: Roast Ribs of Beef, page 65; Potato Nests, page 65

PRALINE LACE CONES

These crisp-crisp cookie cones are equally good served by themselves as tea-time sweets.
Bake at 300° for 10 minutes.
Makes about 3 dozen.

¼ cup (½ stick) butter or margarine, softened
½ cup firmly packed brown sugar
1 egg
¼ cup finely chopped pecans
2 tablespoons flour
¼ teaspoon salt

1. Preheat oven to 300°. Beat butter with sugar in medium-size bowl. Beat in egg until fluffy-light; stir in pecans, flour and salt.
2. Drop batter by half-teaspoonsful, about 5 inches apart, on lightly greased cookie sheet; spread each into a very thin, 2½-inch round. (Make only 2 cookies at a time for easier handling. To save time, shape a batch on aluminum foil while baking a batch. Just slide foil onto cookie sheet.)
3. Bake in a preheated slow oven (300°) for 10 minutes or until golden brown. Cool on cookie sheet 1 minute or just until firm enough to hold their shape.
4. Cut in half with sharp knife, then loosen with spatula. Quickly roll each half into a tiny cone shape; place on wire rack to cool and crisp. (If cookies become too brittle to shape easily, return cookie sheet to oven for 30 seconds to soften.)

Note: Bake and shape about 8 for the pie. Bake remainder as thin, flat cookies without halving.

TRADITIONAL THANKSGIVING DINNER

Oyster Soup*
Roast Turkey*
with Corn Sausage Stuffing*
and Giblet Gravy*
Baked Mashed Potatoes*
Creamed Onions with Lima Beans*
Gingered Carrots*
Double Cranberry Relish Mold*
Apple-Mince Crumb Pie*
Caramel Pumpkin Custard*
Coffee   Hot Tea

*Recipe given

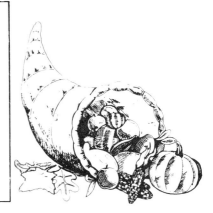

OYSTER SOUP

Makes about 8 cups.

1½ cups finely chopped celery
1½ cups finely chopped green onions
2 cloves garlic, finely chopped
6 tablespoons (¾ stick) unsalted butter
3 tablespoons flour
2 cans (8 ounces each) oysters
3 cans (13¾ ounces each) chicken broth
1 teaspoon salt
⅛ teaspoon cayenne
¼ cup chopped fresh parsley

1. Cook celery, green onions and garlic in butter in a large kettle or Dutch oven until onions are soft. Stir in flour and cook for 2 minutes. Remove kettle from heat.
2. Drain oysters, reserving liquid. Add oyster liquid, chicken broth, salt and cayenne to kettle, stirring until smooth. Bring to boiling; lower heat and simmer 30 minutes.
3. Just before serving, stir in the oysters; heat soup for 3 minutes just until piping hot; sprinkle with parsley.

ROAST TURKEY

Roast at 325° for 3 to 3½ hours.
Makes 12 servings.

1 twelve-pound
 fresh or thawed,
 frozen turkey
Salt and pepper
Corn Sausage
 Stuffing (recipe
 follows)
6 tablespoons (¾
 stick) butter or
 margarine,
 melted

1. Remove turkey neck and giblets and use to make broth for a gravy, if you wish. Rinse turkey under running cold water; pat dry inside and out with paper toweling. Season cavities with salt and pepper.
2. Fill neck cavity loosely with enough Corn Sausage Stuffing to round it out to a plump shape. Skewer skin against backbone. Fill body cavity with remaining stuffing, taking care not to pack stuffing. (It will expand during cooking.) If opening has band or skin or metal clamp across it, push drumsticks under band or clamp. If not, tie legs together and to tail. Twist wing tips under back of turkey.
3. Brush stuffed bird all over with melted butter. Place, breast-side up, on rack in open roasting pan.
4. Roast in a slow oven (325°) for 30 minutes. Brush with butter. During the remaining roasting time, baste every half hour with buttery drippings in bottom of pan. It will take 3 to 3½ hours to cook. A thermometer inserted in center of inside thigh muscle, not touching bone, should register 185°. You can test the bird for doneness by inserting the point of a paring knife into the thickest part of the thigh. The juices should run clear yellow, not pink. If they are pink, continue roasting until they are yellow. The thickest part of the drumstick should feel very soft when pressed between fingers protected by paper towels. The leg should twist easily in its socket.
5. Remove turkey to serving platter. Cover with foil to keep warm. Let stand 20 minutes before carving. Garnish serving platter with watercress, orange wedges and whole mixed nuts, if you wish.

CORN SAUSAGE STUFFING

Makes 10 cups.

1 pound bulk pork sausage 3 medium-size onions, chopped (1½ cups)	8 cups day-old bread cubes (16 slices)	1 tablespoon dried parsley flakes	1½ teaspoons poultry seasoning 1 teaspoon salt	¼ teaspoon pepper 1 can (about 17 ounces) cream-style corn

1. Cook sausage in a large skillet, stirring to break up, until browned. Remove from skillet. Pour off all but ¼ cup sausage fat. (Add vegetable oil if necessary to make ¼ cup.) Cook onions in fat until soft.
2. Combine bread cubes with parsley, poultry seasoning, salt and pepper in a large bowl.

Add onion mixture, sausage and corn and toss until well combined.

Note: If you have any stuffing left after stuffing the turkey, refrigerate. Form into 2-inch balls. Bake in pan around turkey the last 30 minutes of roasting. Place in shallow pan and keep warm in oven until dinner is ready.

GINGERED CARROTS

Carrots are glazed in a buttery sugar mixture spiced with ginger.
Makes 8 servings.

12 medium-size
 carrots, pared
⅓ cup sugar
1 teaspoon ground
 ginger
6 tablespoons (¾
 stick) butter or
 margarine

1. Cut carrots in half lengthwise. Cook, covered, in boiling water until barely tender, 12 to 15 minutes. Drain.
2. Combine sugar and ginger. Roll carrots in sugar mixture. Melt butter in a large skillet. Add carrots. Cook, turning occasionally, until glazed, 10 minutes.

Overleaf: Traditional Thanksgiving Dinner: Creamed Onions with Lima Beans, page 72; Roast Turkey, page 69; Baked Mashed Potatoes, page 72; Gingered Carrots, page 69; Double Cranberry Relish Mold, page 73; Apple-Mince Crumb Pie, page 73; Caramel Pumpkin Custard, page 73

GIBLET
GRAVY

You can make gravy at the last minute by preparing giblets ahead of time, and pre-measuring the flour and broth.
Makes about 5 cups.

Turkey neck and giblets
4 cups water
3 teaspoons or envelopes instant chicken broth
1 teaspoon salt
⅛ teaspoon pepper
1 medium-size onion, chopped (½ cup)
Few celery tops
½ cup fat from turkey, roasting pan
½ cup all-purpose flour

1. Combine turkey neck and giblets (except liver) with water, chicken broth, salt, pepper, onion and celery tops in a large saucepan. Bring to boiling. Lower heat; simmer, covered, 1 hour and 40 minutes. Add liver. Continue simmering 20 minutes or until giblets are tender.
2. Strain broth; measure. Add water if necessary to make 4 cups. Reserve. Chop giblets finely or put through a food grinder. Chill broth and giblets until ready to make gravy.

3. After turkey has been removed from roasting pan, remove rack, if used. Tip pan and let fat rise in one corner. Pour off all fat into a cup, leaving juices in pan. Measure ½ cup fat and return to pan. Blend in flour. Cook, stirring constantly, until blended and bubbly.
4. Stir in giblet broth with giblets. Continue cooking, stirring constantly, scraping browned bits from bottom and sides of pan, until gravy thickens and bubbles. Season with salt and pepper, if needed.

BAKED
MASHED POTATOES

Bake at 325° for 1 hour and 30 minutes.
Makes 8 cups.

3 pounds medium-size potatoes, pared (about 9)
1½ cups dairy sour cream
¼ cup (½ stick) butter or margarine
1½ teaspoons salt
¼ teaspoon pepper
¼ cup packaged bread crumbs
1 tablespoon butter or margarine, melted

1. Cook potatoes in boiling water until tender. Drain thoroughly.
2. Combine potatoes, sour cream, ¼ cup butter, salt and pepper in large bowl. Beat at low speed with electric mixer until blended. Beat at high speed until light and fluffy.
3. Pile lightly into a buttered 2-quart casserole. Cover and refrigerate overnight, if you wish.
4. Bake, covered, in a slow oven (325°) for 1 hour. Toss bread crumbs in 1 tablespoon melted butter. Sprinkle over potatoes. Continue baking, uncovered, 30 minutes.

CREAMED ONIONS
WITH LIMA BEANS

Combine two favorite frozen vegetables for an easy dish.
Makes 8 servings.

1 package (10 ounces) frozen lima beans
2 packages (9 ounces each) frozen small onions with cream sauce
1⅓ cups water
3 tablespoons butter or margarine
½ teaspoon curry powder

1. Cook lima beans in boiling, salted water until barely tender; drain.
2. Combine frozen onions with sauce, water, butter and curry powder. Cover and bring to a full rolling boil over high heat. Lower heat; simmer, covered, 4 minutes, stirring occasionally.
3. Remove from heat. Stir just until sauce is smooth. Stir in beans. Return to low heat until beans are hot, about 3 minutes.

DOUBLE CRANBERRY RELISH MOLD

Makes 10 servings.

1 package (3 ounces) raspberry-flavored gelatin
1 package (3 ounces) lemon-flavored gelatin
½ cup sugar
2 cups boiling cranberry juice cocktail
1 cup cold water
1 can (8 ounces) crushed pineapple in pineapple juice

1 tablespoon lemon juice
2 cups fresh or frozen cranberries

1 unpeeled small orange, quartered and seeded
1 cup chopped celery
½ cup chopped walnuts

1. Combine raspberry and lemon gelatins with sugar in a large bowl. Pour boiling cranberry juice cocktail over, stirring to dissolve. Stir in cold water, undrained pineapple and lemon juice. Chill until as thick as unbeaten egg white.

2. Put cranberries and orange through food grinder. Combine with celery and nuts. Fold into gelatin mixture. Pour into an 8½-cup mold or a 12 × 7½ × 2-inch baking dish. Chill until firm. Unmold onto serving platter. Garnish with celery tops and sugared whole cranberries, if you wish.
Note: To make sugared cranberries, beat 1 egg white slightly; dip cranberries in egg white and roll in sugar. Let dry on paper toweling.

APPLE-MINCE CRUMB PIE

Bake at 425° for 40 minutes.
Makes one 9-inch pie.

2 cups bottled prepared mincemeat
1 nine-inch unbaked pastry shell

3 medium-size apples, pared, cored and sliced (3 cups)
½ cup granulated sugar
1½ tablespoons lemon juice

½ cup all-purpose flour
½ cup firmly packed brown sugar
¼ cup (½ stick) butter or margarine

1. Preheat oven to 425°. Spread mincemeat evenly in pie shell. Toss apples with granulated sugar and lemon juice in a medium-size bowl; spread over mincemeat.
2. Stir flour and brown sugar into medium-size bowl. Cut in butter until coarse crumbs form. Sprinkle over apples.
3. Bake in a preheated hot oven (425°) for 40 minutes.

CARAMEL PUMPKIN CUSTARD

Bake at 325° for 2 hours.
Makes 8 servings.

1 cup sugar
½ cup water
4 eggs, slightly beaten
1 can (16 ounces) pumpkin
½ cup sugar
1 teaspoon ground cinnamon
½ teaspoon ground ginger
½ teaspoon salt
¼ teaspoon ground cloves
1 teaspoon vanilla
1 can (13 ounces) evaporated milk (1⅔ cups)

1. Combine 1 cup sugar and water in a large skillet. Cook over high heat, stirring constantly, until sugar is dissolved. Continue cooking, stirring occasionally, until syrup begins to turn a golden color. Lower heat to medium and stir constantly. When syrup is a light caramel color, pour into a 9-inch pie plate lined with foil. Cool until firm.
2. Remove foil from caramelized sugar and place sugar in plastic bag. Crush with wooden mallet or rolling pin. Butter a 1½-quart baking dish generously. Sprinkle sugar over bottom and side of baking dish.
3. Combine eggs and pumpkin in a large bowl. Blend in remaining ½ cup sugar, cinnamon, ginger, salt, cloves and vanilla. Stir in milk. Pour into caramel sugar-lined baking dish.
4. Place baking dish in a baking pan just large enough to hold it. Pour 1½ inches hot water into pan around baking dish.
5. Bake in a slow oven (325°) for 2 hours or until knife inserted 1 inch from edge comes out clean. Cool; refrigerate. Turn out onto serving platter. Garnish with whipped cream.

Hanukkah: Brisket of Beef with Apricot and Prune Tsimmes, page 76; Dried Fruit Strudel, page 77; Carrot-Nut Cake, page 77

HANUKKAH

A JOYOUS EIGHT-DAY JEWISH HOLIDAY.

Hanukkah, also called the "Feast of Lights," celebrates a military victory for religious liberty by the Jews over 2,000 years ago. After the Jews had driven off their enemy and won back the right to worship in the Holy Temple of Jerusalem, they discovered that the sacred lamp which should burn continuously had gone out. They found enough oil for one day only, but miraculously, it burned for eight days. For that reason, Hanukkah, which means "dedication" in Hebrew, is celebrated for eight days and called the feast of lights. Hanukkah stands for the continual dedication of a people to their religion. The observance begins on the twenty-fifth day of the Hebrew month, Kislev, which is November to December. Each night of the holiday, one candle is lit until, on the eighth night, the menorah is fully aglow. The holiday is especially fun for children because of the festive parties, the gifts which are exchanged each night, the dreidel games and, most of all, the foods kids love. Dreidel is a four-sided top marked with Hebrew letters, N, G, H and S, representing the Yiddish words *nimm* (take), *gib* (give), *halb* (half), and *stell* (put). The letters also stand for a phrase, *Nes Gadol Hayah Sham* (a great miracle came about there). In the dreidel game, using nuts or chocolate coins as exchange, the players put and take according to which side of the top lands up when spun. For this holiday, a hot buffet is usually served. Some favorite dishes include tsimmes, a sweet fruit and vegetable stew served with meat; potato latkes or pancakes; strudel and doughnuts.

HANUKKAH BUFFET

Tahini (Sesame Dip)
Falafel (Fried Mashed Chick-pea Balls)
Brisket of Beef
*Apricot and Prune Tsimmes**
Cucumber, Pepper and Lettuce Salad
Lemon Oil Salad Dressing
*Potato Latkes**
*Cheese Pancakes**
*Dried Fruit Strudel**
*Carrot-Nut Cake**
Turkish Coffee

*Recipe given

BRISKET OF BEEF WITH APRICOT AND PRUNE TSIMMES

Makes 8 servings.

1 brisket of beef or chuck roast (3 pounds) 2 teaspoons salt	¾ teaspoon pepper 1 tablespoon vegetable oil ½ cup boiling water	1 package (12 ounces) pitted prunes 1 package (8 ounces) dried apricots	3 medium-size sweet potatoes, pared and quartered lengthwise	3 tablespoons light brown sugar 2 tablespoons lemon juice 1½ cups boiling water

1. Trim excess fat from meat; rub meat well with salt and pepper; brown in oil in a Dutch oven or heavy saucepan; pour off fat. Add the ½ cup boiling water; cover. Simmer 1 hour.
2. While meat is cooking, soak prunes and apricots in additional warm water to cover in a medium-size bowl. When ready to use, drain.*
3. Add prunes, apricots, sweet potatoes, brown sugar, lemon juice and the 1½ cups boiling water to Dutch oven; cover. Simmer 1½

hours or until meat is tender when pierced with a two-tined fork.

4. To serve: Slice meat; place on heated serving platter; surround with apricots, prunes and sweet potatoes. Skim fat from gravy; pour some over the meat; pass remainder in a gravy boat.

*1½ cups of the soaking liquid may be measured out and used in step 3 instead of the 1½ cups boiling water.

POTATO LATKES

Makes about 24 pancakes.

6 large potatoes, pared 4 eggs, separated 1 large onion, grated 2 teaspoons salt ⅛ teaspoon pepper Dash paprika Vegetable oil for frying	

1. Grate potatoes on a fine grater; place in a large bowl of water. Drain well. Squeeze dry with hands or a potato ricer. Return potatoes to bowl.
2. Beat egg whites in a large bowl until stiff peaks form. Mix potatoes, egg yolks, onion, salt, pepper and paprika. Add egg whites and fold in until well mixed.
3. Pour enough oil into a heavy skillet to make a

depth of ¼ inch; heat. Drop potato mixture, a rounded tablespoon for each cake, into skillet; flatten slightly with back of spoon to make thin pancakes. Fry slowly, turning once, 3 minutes or until crisp and golden. Drain on paper toweling; keep warm. Serve with sour cream or applesauce, if you wish.

CHEESE PANCAKES

Makes about 12 four-inch pancakes.

1½ cups large-curd cottage cheese ½ cup dairy sour cream ½ teaspoon salt 3 eggs, separated 1 cup *sifted* all-purpose flour 6 tablespoons (¾ stick) butter	

1. Combine cheese, sour cream, salt and egg yolks in a medium-size bowl. Stir in flour until well mixed.
2. Beat egg whites in small bowl with electric mixer until stiff peaks form; fold gently into cheese mixture.
3. Melt 2 tablespoons of the butter in large skillet. Drop cheese mixture by scant ⅓ cupfuls

into hot butter (add more butter if needed); flatten with pancake turner to make an even thickness. Cook until golden brown on both sides. Keep warm in slow oven (200°) while cooking remaining pancakes. Serve with sour cream or sprinkle with cinnamon and sugar, if you wish.

DRIED FRUIT STRUDEL

Bake at 400° for 30 minutes.
Makes 16 servings.

- 1 **package (8 ounces) dried apricots**
- 2 **cups (8 ounces) pitted prunes**
- 1 **cup (6 ounces) pitted dates, snipped**
- 1 **medium-size apple, pared, cored and chopped (1 cup)**
- 2 **teaspoons grated lemon rind**
- 3 **tablespoons lemon juice**
- ½ **cup finely chopped walnuts**
- ⅔ **cup granulated sugar**
- 8 **strudel or phyllo leaves (from a 1-pound package)**
- ¾ **cup (1½ sticks) butter or margarine, melted**
- **10X (confectioners') sugar**

1. Soak apricots and prunes in warm water to cover for 15 minutes; drain well. Chop fruits or snip them with scissors.
2. Combine apricots, prunes, dates, apples, lemon rind, lemon juice, walnuts and granulated sugar in a large bowl; mix well.
3. Preheat oven to 400°. Place a clean kitchen towel on a flat working surface; sprinkle lightly with water. Carefully place one strudel or phyllo leaf on towel; brush with butter. Repeat with 3 more strudel leaves and butter. (Keep remaining leaves covered with a moist towel to prevent drying.)
4. Leaving 2-inch margins on sides, spoon half of the fruit mixture in an even row along one long edge; fold in margins.
5. Using the towel to lift dough, roll dough over filling like a jelly roll, using towel to lift and aid rolling. Repeat with remaining strudel leaves and filling for second strudel.
6. Line a large cookie sheet with heavy-duty aluminum foil. Ease filled rolls onto cookie sheet, placing about 3 inches apart; brush each with some of the melted butter. Turn up edges of foil 1 inch all around in case of spills.
7. Bake in a preheated hot oven (400°) for 30 minutes, brushing several times with remaining butter until pastry is golden.
8. Allow pastry to cool 15 minutes and then slide onto serving board. Sprinkle with 10X sugar. Cut each strudel into 8 slices with a sharp knife. Serve warm.

CARROT-NUT CAKE

Bake at 350° for 1 hour.
Makes 8 servings.

- 1 **cup *sifted* all-purpose flour**
- 2 **teaspoons baking powder**
- ⅛ **teaspoon salt**
- ½ **cup vegetable shortening**
- 1 **cup sugar**
- 3 **eggs, separated**
- 1 **cup shredded carrots**
- ½ **cup finely chopped walnuts**
- 2 **tablespoons rum, brandy or orange juice**
- 1 **teaspoon lemon juice**
  Apricot Glaze (*recipe follows*)
  Walnut halves

1. Grease a 2-quart fancy tube pan (or you can use a 9-inch tube pan but cake will not be as high). Dust lightly with flour; tap out excess. Preheat oven to 350°.
2. Sift flour, baking powder and salt onto wax paper.
3. Beat shortening, sugar and egg yolks in a large bowl with electric mixer at high speed for 3 minutes, scraping down side of bowl and beaters occasionally. (Finish mixing cake by hand.)
4. Stir in carrots, walnuts, rum and lemon juice. Stir in flour mixture a little at a time until batter is smooth.
5. Beat egg whites in a small bowl with electric mixer until soft peaks form; fold into cake batter. Spoon into prepared pan, spreading top evenly.
6. Bake in a preheated moderate oven (350°) for 1 hour or until top springs back when lightly pressed with fingertip. Cool in pan on wire rack 10 minutes; loosen cake around edge with a metal spatula; turn out onto a wire rack; cool completely. Brush with Apricot Glaze; garnish with walnut halves.

Apricot Glaze: Heat ⅓ cup apricot preserves in a small skillet; press through a sieve into a small bowl. Brush glaze over top and side of cake.

CHRISTMAS

'TIS THE SEASON OF ICY WEATHER BUT WARM SPIRITS.

Christmas is the most important holiday of the year in Christian countries. People all over the world celebrate the birth of Christ in their own special ways in the weeks leading up to Christmas Day, December 25th. Some people begin the season with Advent, the first Sunday in December and continue the festivities to the feast of the Epiphany on January 6th. Although customs and repasts vary from country to country, Christmas is always a season of warmth, joy and devotion. Parents keep children enchanted with the story of a jolly old man dressed in red, who comes from the North Pole and delivers presents on Christmas Eve. He's really a combination of fact and fiction in the persons of St. Nicholas, Kris Kringle and Santa Claus. St. Nicholas was a bishop who lived during the first half of the 4th century. He became the patron saint of many European people—especially children. He supposedly gave gifts to children when he visited them on the eve of his feast day, December 6th.

> **TRADITIONAL HOLIDAY DINNER**
>
> *B and B Broth**
> *with Mustard Cream Puffs**
> *Roast Goose*
> *White and Wild Rice*
> *Baked Acorn Squash with Creamed Peas*
> *Crisp Vegetable Salad with*
> *Creamy Herb Dressing*
> *Steamed Plum Pudding with Hard Sauce*
> *Walnut Yule Log**
> *with Marzipan "Mushrooms"**
> *Demitasse*
>
> *Recipe given

Through the centuries, St. Nicholas became known as Sinterklass which gradually evolved to Santa Claus. As for his sleigh and reindeer, they originated in the now famous poem "The Night Before Christmas." Most of the Christmas carols originated during the 19th century in Europe and were introduced to America by the English. We've begun this holiday by suggesting a traditional Christmas dinner. It's the most important meal of the day, so plan a festive feast. Recipes that will make your meals extra special have been included, like the B and B Broth with Mustard Cream Puffs. Our second dinner features Stuffed Breast of Turkey Ballottine. You'll take great pride in presenting this dish—it's so pretty on the table . . . and so easy to prepare. If you're planning to entertain a large group, consider our Buffet Open House. You can even bolster your buffet menu with other recipes offered in this section. They're all delicious and all thoroughly tested by us to guarantee perfect results.

B AND B
BROTH

This hot Burgundy-and-beef-broth mixture has a touch of spice and makes a good cold weather "welcome" drink.
Makes 8 six-ounce servings.

2 cans condensed beef broth	1 cup water	Mustard Cream Puffs *(recipe follows)*
2 cups red Burgundy wine	8 whole cloves	

Combine broth, wine, water and cloves in large saucepan. Heat just to boiling; lower heat; cover. Simmer 5 minutes. Ladle or pour into heated punch cups or small mugs. Serve with Mustard Cream Puffs.

MUSTARD
CREAM PUFFS

Airy puffs of golden pastry filled with a mellow mustard cream.
Bake at 400° for 20 minutes.
Makes 32 small cream puffs.

½ cup water
¼ cup (½ stick) butter or margarine
¼ teaspoon salt
½ cup *sifted* all-purpose flour
2 eggs
½ cup heavy cream
1 teaspoon sugar
1 tablespoon Dijon mustard
Finely chopped red radish

1. Preheat oven to 400°. Heat water, butter and salt to a full rolling boil in a small saucepan.
2. Add flour all at once. Stir vigorously with a wooden spoon until mixture forms a thick smooth ball that follows the spoon and leaves the side of pan clean, about 1 minute. Remove from heat; cool slightly.
3. Add eggs, 1 at a time, beating well after each addition, until paste is shiny and smooth. Drop by teaspoonful, 1 inch apart, on ungreased cookie sheet.
4. Bake in a preheated hot oven (400°) for 20 minutes or until puffed and golden. Cool completely on wire rack. *Make-ahead Note:* Freeze in plastic bags until ready to fill and serve.
5. Beat cream with sugar until stiff; fold in mustard.
6. To fill puffs: Cut a slice from top of each puff, then spoon filling in; replace tops loosely so filling shows. Sprinkle chopped radish on filling. Garnish with celery leaves, if you wish.

WALNUT YULE
LOG

The chocolate roll is filled with a coffee and walnut-cream mixture, glazed with chocolate and decorated with marzipan "mushrooms."
Makes 12 servings.

Chocolate Roll *(recipe follows)*
2 egg yolks
2 tablespoons sugar
1 teaspoon cornstarch
½ cup light cream or half-and-half
¾ cup (1½ sticks) unsalted butter
1 cup 10X (confectioners') sugar
1 teaspoon instant coffee powder
1 teaspoon vanilla
1 cup very finely chopped walnuts

¾ cup semisweet chocolate pieces
3 tablespoons unsalted butter or margarine (for glaze)

1 tablespoon milk or cream
Marzipan "Mushrooms" *(recipe follows)* *(optional)*

1. Prepare Chocolate Roll.
2. Combine egg yolks, 2 tablespoons sugar and cornstarch in small saucepan; blend in cream. Cook, stirring constantly, over medium heat, until mixture comes to a boil. Remove from heat; cool; chill.
3. Beat butter in a medium-size bowl with electric mixer until soft and smooth. Beat in 10X sugar until smooth. Dissolve coffee in vanilla;

add to butter mixture. Gradually add chilled egg yolk mixture, 1 tablespoon at a time, while beating constantly. Beat until light and fluffy; fold in nuts.
4. Unroll cake carefully; spread with about ⅔ of walnut mixture. Roll, lifting cake with the end of the towel. Place, seam-side down, on small cookie sheet. Spread remaining walnut mixture over roll. Chill overnight.
5. Melt chocolate pieces with butter and milk in a double boiler over hot, not boiling, water, stirring occasionally until smooth. Let stand 5 minutes, then quickly spread over roll. Sprinkle top with chopped pistachio nuts, if you wish. Keep chilled until serving time. Garnish with Marzipan "Mushrooms," if you wish.

CHOCOLATE ROLL

Bake at 375° for 12 minutes.
Makes one 10-inch roll.

¾ cup *sifted* cake flour
¼ cup unsweetened cocoa powder
1 teaspoon baking powder
3 eggs
¾ cup sugar
3 tablespoons water
1 teaspoon vanilla
10X (confectioners') sugar

1. Grease a 15½ × 10½ × 1-inch jelly-roll pan; line bottom with wax paper; grease paper. Sift flour, cocoa and baking powder onto wax paper.
2. Preheat oven to 375°. Beat eggs in a medium-size bowl with electric mixer until thick and creamy. Gradually add sugar, beating constantly, until mixture is *very* thick. Stir in water and vanilla. Fold in flour mixture. Spread batter in prepared pan.
3. Bake in a preheated moderate oven (375°) for 12 minutes or until center springs back when lightly pressed with fingertip.
4. Loosen cake around edges with a small spatula; invert pan onto clean towel lightly dusted with 10X sugar; peel off wax paper. Starting at one of the short sides, roll cake and towel up together. Place, seam-side down, on wire rack; cool completely.

MARZIPAN "MUSHROOMS"

Shape packaged marzipan into different size "mushrooms." Brush or spread red frosting from a decorating tube over tops, then dip in coarse sugar. Add green food coloring to 1 or 2 tablespoons marzipan to tint a leaf green; flatten small pieces into leaf shapes.

FESTIVE CHRISTMAS DINNER

Smoked Salmon and Cheese Canapés
Stuffed Breast of Turkey Ballottine*
Glazed Carrot Sticks
Buttered Broccoli Spears
Au Gratin Potato Casserole*
Orange and Grape Salad
Savory Cranberry Sauce*
Mincemeat Ice Cream Pie
Dinner Mints

*Recipe given

Overleaf: Festive Christmas Dinner: Stuffed Breast of Turkey Ballottine, page 84; Au Gratin Potato Casserole, page 84; Savory Cranberry Sauce, page 85

STUFFED BREAST OF TURKEY BALLOTTINE

The turkey breast can be boned and the dressing prepared the day before and refrigerated separately, or the stuffed breast can be prepared through step 5 early in the day and held in the refrigerator until 3 hours before serving time.
Makes 12 servings.

½ pound mushrooms
¼ cup (½ stick) butter or margarine
3 packages (10 ounces each) frozen chopped spinach, thawed
3 eggs, beaten
1 teaspoon leaf thyme, crumbled
1 teaspoon salt
¼ teaspoon pepper
1½ cups fresh bread crumbs (about 3 slices)
1 whole turkey breast (about 6½ to 7 pounds), thawed if frozen
1 slice cooked ham, cut about ½-inch thick (½ pound)
2 cans (13¾ ounces each) chicken broth

1½ cups dry white wine
1 large onion, quartered
2 celery stalks, cut into 1-inch pieces
2 carrots, cut into 1-inch pieces
6 peppercorns
1 large bay leaf
Creamy Mustard Gravy (recipe follows)

1. Reserve two mushroom caps for garnish; finely chop remaining mushrooms. Sauté chopped mushrooms in butter in a small skillet just until tender and lightly browned, about 5 minutes.
2. Drain thawed spinach thoroughly, pressing out excess liquid against the side of a strainer. Combine sautéed mushrooms, drained spinach, eggs, thyme, salt, pepper and bread crumbs; mix well. Set aside.
3. Place turkey breast, skin-side down, on board. With a sharp thin-bladed knife, carefully remove breastbone and ribs from meat without piercing the skin; reserve bones. Split through thickest part of breast, but not cutting all the way through; fold out, flatten with hand. (This will give you a larger amount of breast meat to enclose stuffing.)
4. Spoon one-third of the spinach mixture down center of boned breast. Cut ham slice into 6 half-inch-wide strips. Place 3 strips on

dressing. Carefully spoon one-third dressing over ham strips. Repeat with remaining three ham strips and remaining dressing. Fasten overlapped meat with skewers to aid rolling.
5. Wrap skewered breast tightly in cheesecloth. Remove skewers. Tie at 1-inch intervals with string.
6. Place rolled and wrapped turkey breast atop the bones in a Dutch oven or roasting pan. Add chicken broth, wine, onion, celery, carrots, peppercorns and bay leaf. Bring to boiling; lower heat; cover. Simmer, turning once, about 2 hours or until tender and juices from meat run clear with no trace of pink when pierced with a two-tined fork. Cool in broth for 1 hour.
7. Remove turkey breast from broth; unwrap from cheesecloth. Slice and serve with Creamy Mustard Gravy. Serve with buttered broccoli and carrots, if you wish.

Creamy Mustard Gravy: Melt ¼ cup (½ stick) butter or margarine in a medium-size saucepan. Gradually stir in ¼ cup all-purpose flour. Cook, stirring constantly, over medium heat until bubbly; cook 1 minute longer. Gradually stir in 1 cup milk, 1 cup heavy cream and 2 to 3 tablespoons Dijon mustard. Continue to cook over medium heat, stirring constantly, just until sauce thickens, about 5 minutes.

AU GRATIN POTATO CASSEROLE

The casserole may be refrigerated up to several hours at the end of step 4. The baking time should be increased to 45 minutes.
Bake at 350° for 30 minutes.
Makes 8 servings.

3 pounds potatoes
1 medium-size onion, chopped (½ cup)
6 tablespoons butter
6 tablespoons flour
1 teaspoon salt
¼ teaspoon pepper
3 cups milk
1 jar (4 ounces) pimientos
½ cup chopped fresh parsley
Cheese Topping (recipe follows)

1. Pare potatoes; slice thinly. Cook in small amount of boiling water in a large saucepan for 5 minutes; drain.
2. Sauté onion in butter in same large saucepan until tender, about 3 minutes. Stir in flour, salt and pepper until smooth; cook until bubbly, 1 minute. Gradually stir in milk. Cook, stirring constantly, until mixture thickens and bubbles, about 3 minutes. Remove from heat.
3. Drain and chop pimientos, reserving 2 tablespoons for topping. Stir remaining pimientos into sauce along with parsley.

4. Place potato slices in a buttered 2-quart baking dish; pour sauce over top. Stir gently to mix.
5. Bake in a moderate oven (350°) for 15 minutes. Sprinkle with Cheese Topping. Return to oven; bake 15 minutes longer or until browned and bubbly. Garnish with reserved pimientos.

Cheese Topping: Combine 2 tablespoons melted butter, ¼ cup packaged bread crumbs and ¼ cup shredded process American cheese until well blended.

SAVORY CRANBERRY SAUCE

A sophisticated and delicious way with cranberry sauce that can be made 1 or 2 days ahead.
Makes about 3½ cups.

1 package (12 ounces) fresh or frozen cranberries
1 cup sugar
1 cup dry red wine
2 teaspoons cornstarch

1. Combine cranberries, sugar and ¾ cup of the wine in a medium-size saucepan. Cook over medium heat, stirring occasionally, until cranberries just start to pop their skins.

2. Dissolve cornstarch in remaining ¼ cup wine; stir into cranberry mixture. Continue to cook, stirring constantly, just until sauce thickens and bubbles; cool; chill.

BUFFET OPEN HOUSE

Wassail Bowl*
Blue Cheese Mousse Tart*
Smoked Salmon Soufflé*
Vintner's Pot Roast*
Buttered Brussels Sprouts with Chestnuts
Candied Sweet Potatoes
Pickled Green Beans
Buttermilk Biscuits
Chocolate Tortoni*

*Recipe given

WASSAIL BOWL

A traditional punch from medieval England whose name means "good health."
Bake apples at 350° for 10 minutes.
Makes 12 half-cup servings.

2 red Delicious apples
2 whole cloves
2 whole allspice
2 whole cardamom pods, crushed
1 3-inch piece stick cinnamon
1 quart ale
½ teaspoon ground ginger
½ teaspoon ground nutmeg
1 cup sugar
1½ cups dry sherry
3 eggs, separated

1. Core apples; cut crosswise into ¼-inch-thick slices. Place slices in a shallow baking pan.

2. Bake in a moderate oven (350°) for 10 minutes or until apples are tender, but still firm enough to hold their shape; reserve.

3. Tie cloves, allspice, cardamom and cinnamon in a small piece of cheesecloth. Place in a kettle or Dutch oven with 1 cup of the ale, the ginger and nutmeg. Heat very slowly for 20 minutes over low heat (do not allow to boil). Remove spice bag. Stir in remaining ale, ½ cup of the sugar and the sherry. Heat slowly for 20 minutes.

4. Beat egg whites in a large bowl until foamy-white. Slowly beat in remaining ½ cup sugar until soft peaks form.

5. Beat egg yolks in a small bowl until light; fold into beaten whites. Slowly beat hot ale mixture into the eggs until mixture is smooth.

6. Carefully pour the wassail into a heatproof punch bowl; float baked apple slices on top. Serve in heatproof mugs with a cinnamon stick in each, if you wish.

BLUE CHEESE MOUSSE TART

A handsome make-ahead that will make many savory servings.
Makes 16 servings.

2 envelopes unflavored gelatin
¼ cup cold water
1 container (16 ounces) dairy sour cream
8 ounces blue cheese, crumbled

1 container (16 ounces) cottage cheese
1 teaspoon salt
½ teaspoon leaf rosemary, crumbled

½ teaspoon leaf chervil, crumbled
½ teaspoon leaf thyme, crumbled

¼ teaspoon garlic powder
¼ teaspoon pepper
1 cucumber, unpared, scored and thinly sliced
1 jar (2 ounces) red salmon caviar

12 cherry tomatoes, halved
1 bunch green onions, chopped
1 can (4½ ounces) cooked tiny shrimp, drained
Crackers

1. Sprinkle gelatin over cold water in a small saucepan; let stand 5 minutes to soften. Heat over very low heat, stirring just until dissolved.
2. Combine sour cream, blue cheese, cottage cheese, salt, rosemary, chervil, thyme, garlic powder and pepper in the container of an electric blender; cover and whirl until smooth. Pour into a large bowl.
3. Stir dissolved gelatin into cheese mixture until well blended. Turn mousse mixture into an 11-inch fluted tart pan with a removable bottom that has been rinsed with cold water.
4. Chill mousse in refrigerator until firm, about 4 hours or overnight.
5. To serve: Dip pan quickly in and out of hot water just to the rim; wipe pan dry; gently remove ring of pan. Leave mousse on pan bottom; place on chilled serving plate.
6. Decorate top of mousse with circles of cucumber slices, each topped with a small amount of caviar, cherry tomato halves, chopped green onions and shrimp. Serve with crackers.

SMOKED SALMON SOUFFLÉ

Makes 16 servings.

1¼ cups finely chopped onion
2 tablespoons butter
1 pound smoked salmon*
2 packages (8 ounces each) cream cheese
2 tablespoons finely chopped fresh dill
1 cup heavy cream
1 loaf (10 ounces) square dark bread

1. Prepare a 2-cup soufflé dish with a collar: Fold a length of wax paper, long enough to go around dish, in half, lengthwise. Wrap around dish; secure with string. Collar should extend 4 to 5 inches above rim.
2. Sauté onion in butter in a large skillet, stirring occasionally, until tender, about 5 minutes; cool. (Do not allow to brown.)
3. Remove and discard any bones, skin or tough parts from the salmon. Chop salmon finely, then put into a large bowl. Add softened cream cheese; mix well with electric mixer or by hand. Add onion and dill; blend thoroughly. Mixture should be pale pink and very soft.
4. Beat cream in a medium-size bowl until stiff. Fold into salmon mixture. Spoon mixture into prepared dish, smoothing top. Refrigerate for several hours or overnight. Remove collar and decorate with cream cheese rosettes, if you wish. Cut bread slices into 4 smaller squares; serve with salmon.

Make-ahead Tip: Salmon soufflé may be prepared, covered and refrigerated for up to 3 days before serving.
Some markets may carry "lox trimmings," which are less expensive than lox or smoked salmon.

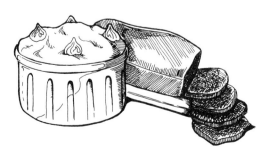

Buffet Open House: Blue Cheese Mousse Tart, page 86; (inset) Chocolate Tortoni, page 88

VINTNER'S POT ROAST

An excellent choice for preparing the day before, then reheating and serving with tender vegetables.
Bake at 325° for 3½ hours.
Makes 12 servings.

1 boneless rolled rump roast (about 5 pounds)	½ teaspoon ground pepper	⅓ cup brandy	2 tablespoons butter or margarine	½ cup chopped carrot
1 teaspoon leaf thyme, crumbled	1 bay leaf	3 tablespoons olive or vegetable oil	1 large onion, chopped (1 cup)	1 celery stalk, chopped
2 cloves garlic, crushed	3 whole cloves	¼ cup all-purpose flour		1 can condensed beef broth
	1 bottle (750 ml.) dry red wine	1 teaspoon salt		

1. Place meat in large glass bowl; add thyme, garlic, pepper, bay leaf, cloves, wine, brandy and oil. Cover and let stand to marinate 4 hours at room temperature or overnight in refrigerator, turning and spooning marinade over meat several times.
2. When ready to cook meat, remove from marinade; pat dry with paper toweling. Rub flour and salt over surface of meat. Brown meat in butter in a heavy kettle or Dutch oven.
3. Meanwhile, heat marinade in large saucepan; boil rapidly 5 minutes to reduce to 2½ cups.
4. Stir onion, carrot and celery into drippings around roast, 5 minutes; add boiling marinade and beef broth. Cover.
5. Bake in a slow oven (325°), turning meat several times, 3½ hours or until meat is tender. Remove meat to a carving board or platter. Remove strings from meat. Keep warm.
6. Strain cooking liquid into a deep bowl, pressing all juices out of the vegetables; discard vegetables. Skim fat from liquid; return liquid to Dutch oven; boil rapidly until reduced to about 3½ cups.* Pour into heated gravy boat and serve with roast.
7. Carve roast into ¼-inch-thick slices. Arrange slices overlapping on platter. Serve with Brussels sprouts, if you wish.

Recipe can be prepared a day ahead up to this point. Return meat to pot; cool and refrigerate. To reheat: Heat meat in its cooking liquid in Dutch oven in a slow oven (325°) about 1 hour or until thoroughly hot.

CHOCOLATE TORTONI

Makes 24 tortoni.

2 squares unsweetened chocolate	1 package (6 ounces) semisweet chocolate pieces	½ cup chopped almonds	4 egg whites	2½ cups heavy cream
		1 container (6½ ounces) candied red cherries	⅛ teaspoon cream of tartar	2 teaspoons sugar
			⅛ teaspoon salt	3 teaspoons vanilla
			¼ cup sugar	

1. Melt the unsweetened chocolate in a 1-cup measure placed in a saucepan with hot, not boiling, water; cool. In a small metal bowl, melt the chocolate pieces over hot water. Toast the almonds in a shallow pan in a moderate oven (350°) for about 10 minutes. Chop enough of the cherries to make 3 tablespoons.
2. Beat egg whites with cream of tartar and salt in a small bowl until foamy-white. Gradually beat in the ¼ cup sugar, 1 tablespoon at a time, until soft peaks form.
3. Beat 2 cups of the cream in a large bowl until stiff. Beat in the remaining 2 teaspoons sugar, the vanilla and melted unsweetened chocolate; blend well.
4. Fold the beaten egg whites, the chopped cherries, toasted almonds and the melted semisweet chocolate into the whipped cream mixture. (Small chunks of chocolate may remain.)
5. Place paper baking cups into 24 muffin-pan cups (about 2¼-inch diameter). Spoon mixture into cups. Freeze until firm, 4 hours or overnight.
6. Beat remaining ½ cup cream in a small bowl until stiff. Garnish each tortoni with a rosette of cream and a candied cherry.

CHRISTMAS BUFFET MENU

Three Vegetable Pâté*
Regal Crown Roast of Pork
with Sweet and Sour Red Cabbage in Apples*
Herb-Seasoned Stuffing
Creamy Baked Onions and Green Beans*
Tray of Crudités: Crisp fennel or celery sticks,
cauliflowerets, radish roses, mushrooms and
olives
Chocolate Amaretto Mousse Pie*
Coffee and Cordials

*Recipe given

THREE
VEGETABLE PÂTÉ

This colorful and unusual appetizer can be made two days ahead.
Bake at 350° for 2 hours.
Makes 12 appetizer servings.

Spinach Layer:
- **2 packages (10 ounces each) frozen chopped spinach**
- **½ cup chopped green onions**
- **2 tablespoons butter or margarine**
- **½ cup light cream**
- **3 eggs, lightly beaten**
- **¼ cup packaged bread crumbs**
- **¼ cup grated Parmesan cheese**
- **½ teaspoon salt**

Mushroom Layer:
- **1 pound mushrooms**
- **1 tablespoon lemon juice**
- **¼ cup (½ stick) butter or margarine**
- **1 large onion, chopped (1 cup)**

- **2 tablespoons dry sherry**
- **1 teaspoon salt**
- **¼ teaspoon pepper**
- **2 eggs, lightly beaten**
- **¼ cup packaged bread crumbs**

Carrot Layer:
- **3 cans (8 ounces each) sliced carrots, drained**

- **2 tablespoons butter**
- **2 tablespoons flour**
- **¼ cup light cream**
- **½ teaspoon salt**
- **¼ teaspoon ground ginger**
- **¼ teaspoon ground nutmeg**
- **2 eggs, lightly beaten**

1. Butter a 9 × 5 × 3-inch loaf pan. Line bottom and ends with foil; butter foil.
2. Prepare Spinach Layer: Cook spinach following label directions; drain and press out excess liquid; chop finely; place in large bowl. Sauté onions in butter in a small skillet 5 minutes; add to spinach. Add cream, eggs, bread crumbs, cheese and salt. Spoon into prepared pan, smoothing surface with spatula or knife.
3. Prepare Mushroom Layer: Trim mushrooms; wipe with damp cloth. Select 6 or 8 perfect mushrooms; toss with lemon juice. Chop remaining mushrooms very finely. Sauté whole mushrooms in butter, turning often, 5 minutes; lift out and arrange in a row lengthwise over spinach in pan. Sauté chopped mushrooms and onion in same skillet until very slightly browned and dry. Stir in sherry, salt and pepper; remove from heat. Blend in eggs and bread crumbs. Spoon mixture over whole mushrooms and spinach layer.
4. Prepare Carrot Layer: Puree carrots until fairly smooth in the container of an electric blender, food processor or through a food mill. Melt butter in medium-size saucepan; stir in flour, cream, salt, ginger, nutmeg and carrots; cook, stirring constantly, until mixture comes to boiling. Remove from heat; beat in eggs all at once. Spoon over mushroom layer. Cover pan with wax paper, then aluminum foil. Set in larger pan; place on oven shelf; pour boiling water into pan to a depth of 1½ to 2 inches.
5. Bake in a moderate oven (350°) for 2 hours or until pâté feels firm to the touch. Transfer loaf pan to a wire rack; cool 1 hour. Refrigerate overnight.
6. Loosen pâté around sides of pan; unmold onto small cookie sheet or plate (peel off foil); turn right-side up onto serving platter. Garnish with fresh mushroom slices and dill or parsley sprigs, if you wish. Serve with crackers or toasted French bread slices.

REGAL CROWN ROAST OF PORK

A spectacular roast filled with your favorite stuffing.
Roast at 425° for 30 minutes, then at 350° for 1 hour and 45 minutes.
Makes 8 servings, plus enough leftovers for a bonus meal.

- 1 **sixteen- or eighteen-chop crown roast of pork, weighing 6 to 7 pounds (give your butcher several days' notice)***
- 1 **teaspoon salt**
- 1 **teaspoon leaf rosemary, crumbled**
- 1 **clove garlic, split**
- 1 **cup chopped celery**
- 1 **medium-size onion, chopped (½ cup)**
- 1 **can (13¾ ounces) chicken broth**
- 3 **tablespoons flour**
  Salt and pepper
  Sweet and Sour Red Cabbage in Apples
  (recipe follows)
  Parsley sprigs

1. Rub roast with salt and rosemary. Place, rib-ends down, in shallow roasting pan. (Ribs form a natural rack.) Insert thermometer into roast so bulb reaches center of meat without touching bone.
2. Roast in hot oven (425°) for 30 minutes. Stir garlic, celery and onion into drippings in pan. Lower oven temperature to 350°. Continue roasting 1 hour and 45 minutes longer or until meat thermometer registers 170° and roast is tender and golden brown.
3. Lift roast to heated serving platter, turning so that ribs are up. Fill center of roast with stuffing, if you wish. Keep warm.
4. Make gravy: Pour chicken broth into roasting pan; heat, stirring with wooden spoon to loosen browned bits. Strain into a 4-cup measure, pressing out all the juices from vegetables; discard vegetables. Skim off excess fat; reserve. Add water to broth mixture to make 2 cups. Measure 3 tablespoons reserved fat into medium-size saucepan; blend in flour; gradually stir in broth mixture. Cook, stirring constantly, until gravy thickens and bubbles 3 minutes. Taste; season with salt and pepper. Serve in heated gravy boat with roast.
5. Garnish platter with Sweet and Sour Red Cabbage in Apples and parsley sprigs. Carve between ribs into serving-size pieces.

If the crown roast comes with a package of ground pork cut from the rib bones, use it in a meat loaf or in meatballs.

Sweet and Sour Red Cabbage in Apples: Drain juice from 1 16-ounce jar of red cabbage; reserve ½ cup. Pour into 13 × 9 × 2-inch baking dish. Add 2 tablespoons red currant jelly. Sauté ½ cup chopped onion in ¼ cup butter or margarine in skillet until tender but not browned, about 8 minutes. Slice tops from 8 baking apples, such as Rome Beauty or Winesap. Remove pulp, discarding cores, to make ½-inch shells. Chop pulp and add to onion mixture; cook and stir 2 to 3 minutes. Stir in drained cabbage. Fill apple shells with cabbage mixture. Place apples in reserved cabbage juice in baking dish. Bake in a moderate oven (350°) for 20 minutes or just until apples are tender. Makes 8 servings.

CREAMY BAKED ONIONS AND GREEN BEANS

Frozen vegetables save you last-minute preparation.
Bake at 350° for 20 minutes.
Makes 8 servings.

- 2 **packages (9 ounces each) frozen cut green beans**
- 1½ **cups water**
- ½ **cup milk**
- ¼ **cup (½ stick) butter or margarine**
- 3 **packages (10 ounces each) frozen creamed onions**
- 3 **tablespoons packaged bread crumbs**
- 3 **tablespoons finely chopped peanuts**

1. Cook beans following label directions; drain.
2. Combine water, milk, butter and frozen onion mixture in a large saucepan. Bring to boiling, stirring often; stir in beans. Pour mixture into a 5- or 6-cup baking dish. Mix bread crumbs and peanuts; sprinkle over top.
3. Bake in a moderate oven (350°) for 20 minutes or until topping is lightly browned.

Christmas Buffet Menu: Three Vegetable Pâté, page 89; Regal Crown Roast of Pork with Sweet and Sour Red Cabbage in Apples, page 91; Creamy Baked Onions and Green Beans, page 91

CHOCOLATE AMARETTO MOUSSE PIE

Makes one 9-inch pie.

1 package (12 ounces) semisweet chocolate pieces
¼ cup (½ stick) butter
1 can (14 ounces) sweetened condensed milk
¼ teaspoon salt
¼ cup water
¼ cup amaretto liqueur
2 cups heavy cream
Sliced almonds for garnish (optional)

1. Line a 9-inch pie plate with aluminum foil; press the foil firmly against the surface of the plate, making the foil as smooth as possible.
2. Melt 1 cup of the chocolate pieces with 2 tablespoons of the butter in small saucepan over very low heat. Pour into foil-lined plate and quickly spread over the bottom and up the side. Place in the freezer until it is firm, about 30 minutes.
3. Meanwhile, prepare filling: Combine remaining chocolate and butter with sweetened condensed milk and salt in medium-size saucepan. Cook, stirring constantly, over low heat until chocolate is melted. Stir in water gradually. Cook, stirring constantly, over medium heat, 5 minutes.
4. Add amaretto; cook and stir again for 5 minutes or until thickened. Cool to room temperature. To hasten cooling, place pan over ice and water, stirring occasionally, for 10 minutes or until cooled.
5. Beat cream in a medium-size bowl until stiff. Remove and refrigerate ½ cup for garnish. Stir a part of the 1½ cups of the whipped cream briskly into chocolate mixture to loosen slightly; fold in remainder.
6. When chocolate shell is firm, lift gently from pan with foil. Carefully peel off foil and place shell on serving plate. Spoon the filling into the shell; garnish with the sliced almonds and reserved whipped cream. Chill until set, about 3½ hours.

CHRISTMAS BRUNCH

Brunch Punch*
Gruyere Gougere*
Chicken Breasts with Almonds*
Baked Rice*
Orange Salad*
Coffee

*Recipe given

BRUNCH PUNCH

Makes 6 servings.

1 can (6 ounces) frozen pineapple-orange juice concentrate
6 ounces vodka
6 ounces apricot or peach brandy
¾ cup cracked ice
1 bottle (28 ounces) club soda, chilled

Combine pineapple-orange concentrate, vodka, brandy and cracked ice in blender container. Cover and blend until smooth. Pour into large stemmed glasses and fill with club soda.

GRUYÈRE GOUGERE

Bake at 375° for 45 minutes.
Makes 6 servings.

1 cup milk
¼ cup (½ stick) butter
½ teaspoon salt
1 cup *sifted* all-purpose flour
4 eggs
4 ounces Gruyère or Swiss cheese, shredded (1 cup)

1. Heat milk, butter and salt in large saucepan until mixture comes to boil.
2. Add flour all at once and stir rapidly over medium heat until mixture is smooth and forms a ball.
3. Empty dough into bowl of an electric mixer and beat in eggs, 1 at a time, until paste is smooth and shiny. Beat in half the cheese.
4. Preheat oven to 375°. Spoon mounds of dough onto greased cookie sheet, forming an 8-inch circle. Each mound should just touch the next, using about ¾ of the paste. With remaining paste, place a small mound on top of each large one.
5. Sprinkle mounds with remaining cheese.
6. Bake in a preheated moderate oven (375°) for 45 minutes or until ring is golden brown.

CHICKEN BREASTS WITH ALMONDS

Bake at 350° for 25 to 30 minutes.
Makes 6 servings.

3 **whole chicken breasts, halved and boned**	½ **cup slivered blanched almonds**	1 **tablespoon chopped green onion**	1 **cup chicken broth**	**Dash nutmeg**
3 **tablespoons butter or margarine**	2 **tablespoons brandy**	1 **teaspoon tomato paste**	¼ **cup white wine or dry vermouth**	¼ **teaspoon pepper**
		2 **tablespoons flour**	¼ **teaspoon salt**	½ **teaspoon leaf tarragon, crumbled**

1. Wash chicken breasts and pat dry.
2. Melt butter in skillet over moderate heat; add almonds and cook, stirring, until almonds begin to brown. Remove with slotted spoon to paper toweling; reserve.
3. Brown chicken breasts lightly on both sides in same skillet over medium heat. Pour brandy over and set aflame. When flame burns out, remove chicken to shallow baking dish. Add onion to juices remaining in skillet; cook over low heat for 30 seconds, stirring constantly. Stir in tomato paste and flour. Gradually stir in chicken broth and white wine and cook, stirring, until sauce is slightly thickened and bubbles. Add salt, nutmeg, pepper and tarragon. Pour over chicken in baking dish. Cover dish with foil.
4. Bake in a moderate oven (350°) for 25 to 30 minutes.
5. Sprinkle sautéed almonds over chicken in baking dish.

Note: To make ahead, cool; re-cover with foil and refrigerate until ready to heat. Reheat, covered, in a moderate oven (350°) for 30 minutes or until sauce is bubbly-hot.

BAKED RICE

Bake at 350° for 30 minutes.
Makes 6 servings.

¼ **cup (½ stick) butter or margarine, softened**	1½ **cups uncooked long-grain rice**	3 **cups chicken broth (or part broth and part water)**
	Dash liquid hot pepper seasoning	1 **bay leaf**

1. Put butter, rice, pepper seasoning, broth and bay leaf in a 1½-quart cook-and-serve casserole with a tight-fitting lid. Bring to boiling; cover dish tightly.
2. Bake in a moderate oven (350°) for 30 minutes.
3. Remove from oven. If kept tightly covered, it will remain hot for 30 minutes, if necessary. Fluff up with fork just before serving. Discard bay leaf. Sprinkle with chopped parsley, if you wish.

ORANGE SALAD

Makes 6 servings.

½ **head Boston lettuce, torn in pieces**	1 **green pepper, seeded and diced**	1 **tablespoon lemon or lime juice**
2 **large oranges, peeled and sliced**	1 **sweet red onion, peeled and diced**	3 **tablespoons vegetable oil**
1 **cucumber, pared and thinly sliced**	½ **teaspoon salt**	
	¼ **teaspoon freshly ground pepper**	

1. Arrange crisp lettuce leaves on individual salad plates; then orange slices and cucumber slices on the lettuce. Top with green pepper and onion.
2. Combine salt, pepper, lemon juice and vegetable oil in a screw-top jar; cover and shake well; pour over salad.

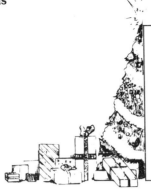
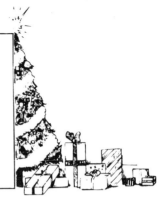

TREE-TRIMMING DESSERT PARTY

Assorted Cheese and Fruit
Kentucky Bluegrass Fudge Pie*
Dobos Torte*
Bourbon Fruitcake*
Swedish Rosettes*
Raspberry-Almond Petit Fours*
Hot Chocolate
Eggnog

*Recipe given

DOBOS TORTE

Thin layers of tender sponge cake are spread with chocolate butter cream and topped with crackly brandy-cream-filled lace cookies. The popular original was created by Hungarian pastry chef Josef Dobos almost 100 years ago.
Bake at 350° for 12 minutes.
Makes 12 servings.

5 **eggs, separated**	4 **squares**	2 **egg yolks**	½ **cup light cream**	**Lace Cookies**
⅔ **cup granulated**	**unsweetened**	2½ **to 3 cups** *sifted*	**or half-and-half**	*(recipe follows)*
sugar	**chocolate**	**10X**	1 **tablespoon**	**Brandy Cream**
1 **teaspoon vanilla**	1 **cup (2 sticks)**	**(confectioners')**	**vanilla**	*(recipe follows)*
⅔ **cup** *sifted* **cake**	**butter or**	**sugar**		
flour	**margarine,**			
	softened			

1. Grease and line two 15½ × 10½ × 1-inch jelly-roll pans with wax paper; grease paper.
2. Beat egg whites in large bowl with electric mixer at high speed until foamy. Sprinkle in ⅓ cup of the sugar, 1 tablespoon at a time, until meringue forms soft peaks. Preheat oven to 350°.
3. With same beaters, beat the egg yolks in a small bowl with remaining sugar and vanilla until thick and fluffy; fold in flour. Stir in ⅓ of the egg white meringue; fold mixture into remaining meringue. Spread batter into prepared pans, dividing evenly; smooth tops.
4. Bake in a preheated moderate oven (350°) for 12 minutes or until center springs back when lightly touched with fingertip. Invert onto wire racks or clean towels; peel off wax paper; cool completely. Cut each cake crosswise into 4 strips, each about 10 × 4-inches.
5. Melt chocolate in the top of a double boiler over hot, not boiling, water. Remove from heat; beat in butter and egg yolks until well blended. Beat in 10X sugar alternately with cream until filling is smooth and spreadable. Stir in 1 tablespoon vanilla.
6. Chill briefly if too soft. Trim layers, if necessary, and stack (8 in all) on serving plate using a slightly rounded ¼ cup of filling between each layer. Smooth remaining filling on sides and top.
7. Prepare Lace Cookies. Arrange about 12 on top of torte. Pipe Brandy Cream into ends of cookies and in small rosettes around base of torte. Chill several hours or overnight.

Tree-Trimming Dessert Party: Dobos Torte, page 94

LACE COOKIES

Bake at 375° for 5 minutes.
Makes about 15.

¼ **cup ground blanched almonds**
¼ **cup sugar**
¼ **cup (½ stick) butter**
1 **tablespoon flour**
1 **tablespoon milk**

1. Preheat oven to 375°. Combine almonds, sugar, butter, flour and milk in small saucepan. Heat, stirring constantly, just until butter is melted and mixture is smooth. Drop by teaspoonsful, 4 inches apart, onto buttered and floured cookie sheets. Work with only 4 or 5 cookies at a time.
2. Bake in a preheated moderate oven (375°) for 5 minutes or until lacy and golden brown. Cool briefly on cookie sheet, then working quickly, turn upside down with spatula and quickly roll around the handle of a wooden spoon. If cookies cool too fast and are too brittle to work with, return to warm oven for a few minutes. Slide off handle onto a wire rack.

Brandy Cream: Beat ¼ cup (½ stick) softened butter with ⅔ cup *sifted* 10X (confectioners') sugar and 2 teaspoons brandy in a small bowl until smooth.

SWEDISH ROSETTES

These crispy star-shaped cookies are made on a special rosette iron and plunged into deep fat to brown.
Makes about 3 dozen.

1 **cup *sifted* all-purpose flour**
2 **tablespoons granulated sugar**
½ **teaspoon salt**
2 **eggs**
1 **cup milk**
2 **tablespoons vegetable oil**
1 **teaspoon vanilla**
Vegetable oil for frying
10X (confectioners') sugar

1. Sift flour, granulated sugar and salt into a medium-size bowl.
2. Beat eggs, milk, the 2 tablespoons oil and vanilla in a small bowl until blended. Stir into flour mixture until batter is smooth.
3. Pour enough oil in a medium-size saucepan to fill half full; heat to 400° on a deep-fat frying thermometer.
4. Heat rosette iron in hot oil for 30 seconds; remove and shake off excess oil. Dip hot iron into batter just up to rim; immerse in hot oil. Leave iron immersed in oil until rosette begins to brown, so it will hold its shape. Shake rosette off iron; turn over; brown on other side. Lift out rosette with a slotted spoon; drain on paper toweling; cool. Repeat with remaining batter. Rosettes may be stored in tightly covered container for up to 2 weeks. Sprinkle with 10X sugar before serving.

KENTUCKY BLUEGRASS FUDGE PIE

Bake at 350° for 30 minutes.
Makes 8 servings.

⅔ **cup *sifted* all-purpose flour**
½ **cup unsweetened cocoa powder**
¼ **teaspoon salt**
1½ **cups coarsely chopped walnuts**
½ **cup (1 stick) butter, softened**
1 **cup sugar**
2 **eggs**
3 **teaspoons vanilla**
1 **pint vanilla ice cream *(optional)***

1. Grease an 8 × 1½-inch layer cake pan. Preheat oven to 350°.
2. Combine flour, cocoa and salt on wax paper.
3. Spread walnuts in a shallow pan. Toast in a moderate oven (350°), stirring often, for 10 minutes; cool; reserve.
4. Beat butter, sugar, eggs and vanilla in a medium-size bowl until light and fluffy. Stir in flour mixture until well blended. Stir in toasted walnuts. Turn into prepared pan.
5. Bake in a preheated moderate oven (350°) for 30 minutes or until a wooden pick inserted in the center comes out with moist crumbs. *Do not overbake.* Cool on wire rack. Remove from pan. Spoon ice cream onto center of pie; garnish with walnut halves, if you wish. Cut into pie-shaped wedges to serve.

BOURBON FRUITCAKE

Old-fashioned pound cake with fruit.
Bake at 300° for 2 hours and 10 minutes.
Makes one 10-inch tube cake.

1½ **cups raisins**
1 **container (8 ounces) mixed candied fruits**
⅓ **cup bourbon**
3½ **cups *sifted* all-purpose flour**
1½ **teaspoons baking powder**
¾ **teaspoon ground nutmeg**
1½ **cups (3 sticks) butter or margarine**
1¾ **cups sugar**
6 **eggs**
⅓ **cup milk**
1½ **cups pecans or walnuts, coarsely chopped**
Bourbon

1. Combine raisins, candied fruits and ⅓ cup bourbon in a medium-size bowl. Let stand at room temperature several hours.
2. Grease a 10-inch tube pan. Dust with flour; tap out excess. Sift flour, baking powder and nutmeg onto wax paper.
3. Preheat oven to 300°. Beat butter in a large bowl until soft; add sugar and beat with electric mixer on high speed until smooth and fluffy. Add eggs, 1 at a time, beating after each addition until light and fluffy.
4. Stir in flour mixture alternately with milk, beating until smooth after each addition. Stir in fruits and nuts. Turn into prepared pan.
5. Bake in a preheated slow oven (300°) for 2 hours and 10 minutes or until top springs back when lightly pressed with fingertip. Cool in pan on wire rack 20 minutes. Loosen around tube and side with a small spatula; turn out of pan onto wire rack; cool completely.
6. Wrap cake in cheesecloth that has been soaked in about ⅓ cup bourbon. Then wrap tightly in foil. Store in refrigerator. Re-soak cheesecloth as it dries out, about once a week. Store cake 3 to 4 weeks to develop flavor. Decorate the top of the cake with candied fruits and nuts, if you wish.

RASPBERRY-ALMOND PETIT FOURS

There is a moist, tender, almond pound cake in the center of these colorful little morsels.
Bake at 325° for 45 minutes.
Makes 4 dozen.

2½ **cups *sifted* cake flour**
1 **teaspoon baking powder**
½ **cup almond paste (not almond filling or marzipan) (from an 8-ounce can or package)**
⅔ **cup butter, softened**
1¼ **cups sugar**
4 **eggs**
½ **cup milk**
Raspberry Glaze (recipe follows)
2 **containers (16.5 ounces each) vanilla ready-to-spread frosting**
Red food coloring
2 **tubes red cake decorating gel**
2 **tubes green cake decorating gel**

1. Butter a 13×9×2-inch pan; line bottom with wax paper; butter paper.
2. Preheat oven to 325°. Sift flour and baking powder onto wax paper.
3. Crumble almond paste into a large bowl; add butter. Beat with electric mixer until creamy and smooth. Beat in sugar and eggs until mixture is fluffy and light, about 3 minutes.
4. Add flour mixture alternately with milk, beating after each addition with mixer at low speed, until batter is smooth. Pour into prepared pan.
5. Bake in a preheated slow oven (325°) for 45 minutes or until center springs back when lightly pressed with fingertip. Cool in pan on wire rack 10 minutes. Loosen around edges with small spatula; turn out onto wire rack; cool completely.
6. Trim top of cake with a large knife to make top flat and even. Cut cake into 48 rectangles, each about 2×1-inches (12 across, 4 down).
7. Prepare Raspberry Glaze. Hold cakes, 1 at a time, on a fork over saucepan of glaze. Dip to evenly coat top and sides. Place cakes on wire rack over wax paper to catch any drips. Let stand until sticky-firm, about 1 hour.
8. Spoon vanilla frosting into top of double boiler; place over simmering water. Heat, stirring occasionally, just until frosting is melted. Stir in a few drops of red food coloring to tint a pale pink.
9. Holding glazed cakes, 1 at a time on a fork, spoon frosting over to coat top and sides, letting excess drip back into pan. Use a wooden pick to slide each cake onto a wire rack. Let stand until frosting is set. Decorate with decorating gels.

Raspberry Glaze: Combine 2 jars (10- to 12-ounces each) red raspberry preserves (about 2 cups), ¼ cup sugar and ¼ cup water in a medium-size saucepan. Bring to boiling; lower heat; simmer 5 minutes, stirring often. Press through sieve to remove seeds; cool slightly.

SPECIAL OCCASIONS

BABY SHOWER

Surprise a mother-to-be with a festive afternoon shower. Close friends of the expectant mother should plan the activity as a cooperative effort. By letting everyone in on the planning, there's less work for one individual. One friend can take care of the party site, another the invitations and table setting, another coordinates the menu and assigns the dishes for each friend to make and bring. Everyone helps with the final clean up. When selecting a shower menu, avoid spicy foods which might not agree with the expectant mother. Choose colorful finger foods that can be made ahead. Guests can enjoy dainty sandwiches and desserts from a buffet table.

BABY SHOWER BUFFET TEA
Miniature Salmon Eclairs*
Deviled Ham Leaves*
Daisy Sandwiches*
Mushroom-Butter Rounds*
Corned Beef Ribbons*
Petit Chocolate Rolls*
Spritz Cookies
Marzipan Fruits*
Party Mints
Three-Fruit Punch*
Coffee   Tea
*Recipe given

MINIATURE SALMON ECLAIRS
Bake at 400° for 25 minutes.
Makes 32 eclairs.

- **½ cup water**
- **¼ cup (½ stick) butter or margarine**
- **½ cup *sifted* all-purpose flour**
- **⅛ teaspoon salt**
- **2 eggs**
  Salmon Salad *(recipe follows)*
  Tiny pickled onions
  Watercress

1. Heat water and butter to boiling in a medium-size saucepan. Add flour and salt all at once; stir vigorously with a wooden spoon 2 minutes or until batter forms a thick smooth ball that follows spoon around pan; remove from heat.
2. Beat in eggs, 1 at a time, until batter is shiny-smooth. Divide in half; place each half on a sheet of wax paper.
3. Preheat oven to 400°. Butter hands; shape batter into logs, 8 inches long and 1½ inches in diameter. Cut each into 16 pieces with a buttered sharp knife. Place, 1 inch apart, on ungreased cookie sheets.
4. Bake in a preheated hot oven (400°) for 25 minutes or until puffed and lightly golden. Remove at once from cookie sheets to wire racks; cool completely.
5. Cut a thin slice from top of each eclair with a sharp knife; scoop out any bits of soft dough from bottoms. Fill bottoms

with Salmon Salad; replace tops. Garnish each with a pickled onion and watercress threaded onto a wooden pick.
Salmon Salad: Drain liquid from 1 can (7¾ ounces) salmon; flake in a medium-size bowl. Fold in 1 cup finely diced unpared zucchini, ¼ teaspoon salt, ⅓ cup mayonnaise or salad dressing and 2 teaspoons lemon juice. Makes about 1½ cups.
Note: Bake eclairs a day or two ahead, if you wish, and store in a loosely covered container. Before filling, re-crisp in a hot oven (400°) for 2 minutes. Filling, too, may be made several hours ahead, then drained and put into shells about an hour before serving.

DEVILED HAM LEAVES
Makes 32 small sandwiches.

- **32 slices white bread (about 2 one-pound loaves)**
- **2 cans (4½ ounces each) deviled ham**
- **3 containers (4 ounces each) whipped cream cheese**
  Green food coloring

1. Cut two leaf shapes from each slice of bread with a 1½-inch-long leaf-shaped or oval cookie cutter.
2. Blend deviled ham and 2 containers of the cream cheese until smooth in a medium-size bowl; spread on bread cut-outs and sandwich to make 32 sandwiches.

3. Blend remaining cream cheese with a few drops food coloring to tint pale green in a small bowl.

4. Fit a plain tip onto a pastry bag; fill with cheese mixture. Press out onto tops of sandwiches to resemble markings on leaves.

Note: Sandwiches may be made up and decorated about an hour ahead. Place in a single layer on a cookie sheet or tray, cover tightly to keep them from drying out, and chill until serving time.

DAISY SANDWICHES

Makes 32 small sandwiches.

1½ dozen hard-cooked eggs
¾ cup mayonnaise or salad dressing
1½ teaspoons prepared mustard
64 slices white bread (about 4 one-pound loaves)

1. Cut eggs in half; scoop out yolks. Press yolks through a fine sieve into a medium-size bowl. (Save whites to dice and cream for a family meal.) Blend mayonnaise and mustard into yolks.

2. Cut 64 flower shapes from bread with a 2½-inch flower-shaped cookie cutter.

3. Measure ½ cup of the yolk mixture and set aside for garnish. Spread remainder on bread cutouts; sandwich to make 32 sandwiches. Top the center of each flower with a dot of reserved yolk mixture.

Note: Sandwiches may be made and decorated about an hour ahead. Place in a single layer on a cookie sheet or tray, cover tightly to keep them from drying out, and chill until serving time.

MUSHROOM-BUTTER ROUNDS

Makes 32 small sandwiches.

¾ cup (1½ sticks) butter or margarine
¾ cup chopped watercress
¼ teaspoon salt
16 slices cracked-wheat bread (about 1 one-pound loaf)
8 medium-size mushrooms, sliced lengthwise
2 tablespoons lemon juice
1 jar (4 ounces) whole pimientos, drained

1. Blend butter, watercress and salt in a small bowl.

2. Cut 2 rounds from each slice of bread with a 1½-inch round cookie cutter to make 32 in all; spread with watercress butter. Brush mushroom slices with lemon juice to keep them white; place one on each buttered bread round.

3. Slit pimientos down side and open out flat, then cut out tiny leaf shapes with a miniature canapé cutter; place 2 around mushroom stems on bread rounds.

Note: Watercress butter may be spread on bread at least an hour ahead. Place sandwiches in a single layer on a cookie sheet or tray; cover tightly to prevent drying, and chill. Cut pimiento leaves ahead and chill until ready to place on sandwiches at serving time. Slice mushrooms just before serving, as they tend to darken on standing.

CORNED BEEF RIBBONS

These layered, pink-and-white-striped sandwiches look attractive on any buffet table.

Makes 32 sandwiches.

1 can (4½ ounces) corned beef spread
1 tablespoon chopped dill pickle
1 tablespoon prepared horseradish
2 tablespoons dairy sour cream
12 slices white bread

1. Mix corned beef spread, pickle, horseradish and sour cream in medium-size bowl. Spread evenly on 8 slices of bread, leaving remaining 4 slices unspread. Make 4 stacks of 2 spread slices (spread-side up) and 1 unspread slice each. Wrap in plastic bags or wax paper. Refrigerate overnight or until serving time.

2. To serve, trim off crusts; cut each sandwich into four strips; cut strips crosswise to make 8 little sandwiches.

PETIT CHOCOLATE ROLLS

Bake at 400° for 8 minutes.
Makes 2½ dozen rolls.

½ cup *sifted* cake flour
¼ cup unsweetened cocoa powder
¾ teaspoon baking powder
¼ teaspoon salt
3 eggs
½ cup sugar
1 teaspoon rum flavoring or extract
10X (confectioners') sugar
1 container (4 ounces) whipped cream cheese
½ cup maraschino cherries, chopped
1 teaspoon maraschino-cherry syrup

1. Grease a 15½ × 10½ × 1-inch jelly-roll pan; line bottom with wax paper; grease paper.

2. Place flour, cocoa, baking powder and salt into sifter.

3. Preheat oven to 400°. Beat eggs until foamy-light and double in volume in a large bowl; beat in sugar, 1 tablespoon at a time, until thick; stir in rum flavoring or extract.

4. Sift flour mixture over top, then fold in; pour into prepared pan.

5. Bake in a preheated hot oven (400°) for 8 minutes or until center springs back when lightly pressed with fingertip. Loosen cake around edges with a knife; invert onto a large cutting board or cookie sheet lightly dusted with 10X sugar; peel off wax paper. Trim crisp edges from cake.

6. Cut cake crosswise into sixths, then lengthwise into fifths; roll up each piece, jelly-roll fashion; wrap tightly in wax paper. Cool completely on a wire rack.

7. Blend cream cheese, cherries and syrup in a small bowl.

8. Unwrap each piece of cake, then unroll and spread with cheese mixture; reroll; chill. Just before serving, sprinkle rolls with 10X sugar.

MARZIPAN "FRUITS"

Makes about 3 pounds.

2 cans (8 ounces each) almond paste
1 jar (7 ounces) marshmallow creme
¼ cup light corn syrup
½ teaspoon almond extract
6 cups *sifted* 10X (confectioners') sugar (about 1½ packages)
Assorted food colorings

1. Crumble almond paste into a large bowl. Add marshmallow creme, corn syrup and almond extract. Beat with electric mixer until well blended. Gradually beat in 2 cups of the sugar until mixture is smooth.

2. Turn mixture out onto a surface dusted with 10X sugar. Knead in remaining sugar until a soft dough is formed.

3. Shape marzipan into assorted fruit shapes. Let stand several hours or overnight for surfaces to dry.

4. Paint shapes with food coloring diluted with water to resemble fruits; let dry several hours or overnight.

THREE-FRUIT PUNCH

Makes 7 cups.

1 can (6 ounces) frozen orange juice concentrate
2½ cups water
1 can (12 ounces) apricot nectar
1 can (18 ounces) pineapple juice

Prepare orange juice concentrate with water in a large pitcher. Stir in apricot nectar and pineapple juice; chill. Pour over ice in glasses.

SOME QUICK TRICKS
WITH PARTY SANDWICHES

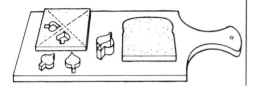

An easy decorating trick for party sandwiches: Use breads of contrasting colors and mark each slice in triangles. Then, using canapé cutters, make tiny cutouts; fit white cutouts into brown bread and vice versa.

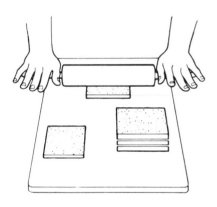

To keep the slices of bread from cracking as they are rolled, flatten each slice first with a rolling pin. Work with only a few slices of bread at a time to keep them from drying out.

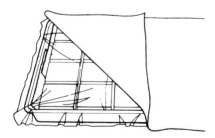

To keep party sandwiches fresh and moist until serving time, arrange the sandwiches in a shallow baking pan lined with damp paper toweling, then cover with a clean towel or plastic wrap and refrigerate until party time.

SPECIAL BIRTHDAY

Just because the birthday candles total more than twenty-one, there's no reason to stop celebrating that special day. You may not care for a decorated birthday cake served with ice cream but how about having an ice cream cake frosted with whipped cream. You can insert a symbolic candle on top and invite your friends for a come-for-dessert birthday party.

COME-FOR-DESSERT PARTY
Fruit with Eggnog Sauce*
Snowball Ice Cream Cake*
Chocolate Lace Roll-ups*
Demitasse or Herb Tea
*Recipe given

FRUIT WITH EGGNOG SAUCE

Jewel-like fruits are complemented by a creamy, bourbon-spiked sauce.
Makes 10 servings.

 3 small fresh pears
 1 can (20 ounces) pineapple slices in pineapple juice, drained
 3 navel oranges, peeled and sliced
 1 can (17 ounces) figs, drained
 Mixed candied fruits
 Eggnog Sauce
 (recipe follows)

1. Wash, halve and core pears; cut into thin wedges; sprinkle with juice from pineapple. Arrange pears and pineapple slices in serving bowl or compote. Fill center with orange slices and figs. Sprinkle mixed candied fruits over top.
2. Chill, covered, until serving time. Serve Eggnog Sauce separately to spoon over each serving.

EGGNOG SAUCE

Makes 2 cups.

 3 egg yolks
 3 tablespoons 10X (confectioners') sugar
 ⅓ cup bourbon or brandy
 ½ cup heavy cream, whipped
 Ground nutmeg

1. Beat egg yolks and sugar in a small bowl with electric mixer until very light and fluffy. Heat bourbon in small saucepan just until bubbles appear around the edge; do not allow to boil. Pour into egg yolk mixture, beating constantly until sauce is well mixed and thickened. Cover and chill several hours.
2. Fold in whipped cream and a dash of nutmeg before serving. Sprinkle additional nutmeg over top.

SNOWBALL ICE CREAM CAKE

Listen for the oohs and ahs when you set this spectacular dessert on the table. No one will ever guess just how easy it was to make!
Makes 16 servings.

 ½ cup slivered almonds
 ⅔ cup sugar
 1 package (10¾ ounces) frozen chocolate pound cake, partially thawed
 2 quarts vanilla ice cream
 2 cups heavy cream
 ¼ cup 10X (confectioners') sugar
 Candied lilacs or violets
 OR: Candied fruits

1. Spread almonds in small skillet; heat over medium heat, stirring or shaking pan often, until lightly toasted, about 10 minutes. Remove almonds from skillet; reserve.
2. Add sugar to skillet; heat slowly until sugar melts and starts to turn golden in color. Stir in almonds; cook and stir over medium heat, 1 minute. Pour mixture onto lightly buttered cookie sheet. Cool completely. Chop coarsely with large knife.
3. Cut cake lengthwise into about 12 very thin slices; cut each long slice in half crosswise. Line two identical 5- or 6-cup round-bottomed mixing bowls with cake slices, overlapping slices to fit. Place in freezer.
4. Remove 1 quart ice cream from freezer; soften slightly in large bowl. Fold in half of almond mixture. Spoon into one cake-lined bowl. Place in freezer. Repeat with remaining ice cream, almond mixture and second bowl. (If you have only one bowl, make and freeze one half; remove from bowl; keep frozen; repeat with other half.)
5. When both "halves" are almost frozen, trim cake to same level as ice cream. Unmold one cake from one bowl and set it on top of the other in second bowl to form a ball. Wrap and freeze several days or weeks until ready to frost and serve.
6. Loosen cake from bowl and unmold ball onto serving plate. Whip the cream with 10X sugar until stiff. Spread a very thin coating over entire ball, then pipe small rosettes of remaining cream close together to cover completely. Decorate with candied flowers or candied fruits. Return to freezer until serving time.
7. When ready to serve, hold cake with a fork while slicing into wedges with large knife.

CHOCOLATE LACE ROLL-UPS

Fragile, crisp little delicacies.
Bake at 325° for 8 minutes.
Makes about 2 dozen.

- **½ cup *sifted* all-purpose flour**
- **¼ cup ground blanched almonds**
- **¼ cup light corn syrup**
- **1 square unsweetened chocolate**
- **¼ cup sugar**
- **¼ cup (½ stick) butter**
- **½ teaspoon vanilla**

1. Combine flour and almonds on wax paper. Preheat oven to 325°.
2. Combine corn syrup, chocolate, sugar and butter in a small saucepan. Cook, stirring constantly, until mixture comes to boiling and chocolate is melted. Remove from heat; stir in vanilla. Stir in flour mixture gradually until well blended.
3. Drop cookie mixture by scant teaspoonful onto ungreased cookie sheets, placing rounds about 3 inches apart. Bake no more than 6 at a time for easier rolling.
4. Bake in a preheated slow oven (325°) for 8 minutes. Remove from oven to wire rack; cool 30 seconds. Scoop up warm cookie with a large metal spatula. Quickly roll around handle of a wooden spoon, holding for a few seconds until cookie stiffens. Transfer to a wire rack to cool. If cookies should become too stiff before rolling, return them to oven for a few minutes to soften. Store in a tightly covered container.

HOME WEDDING RECEPTION

A wedding reception at home can be as successful and lavish an affair as one at a restaurant or hotel. You can successfully "cater" your own reception as long as you prepare carefully and plan everything to the last detail. Enlist the help of family and friends. When preparing foods for a very large group, ordinary recipes serving 6 to 8 cannot simply be multiplied to feed 50. However, prepare the same dish several times and keep them on hold. Replenish the buffet table with them as needed. The time of the wedding determines the type of reception foods to be served. You can have a breakfast reception, a luncheon reception just for the wedding party and immediate family, or a large-scale affair in the evening for all the invited guests. For a very simple reception, you can serve a wedding cake with champagne and snacks. For an elaborate affair, serve a number of appetizers, several main dishes and salads with a champagne punch and cake.

BEST FOODS TO SERVE

- Finger and non-dripping fork foods are easiest to serve and eat—especially when there are many guests and little elbowroom for maneuvering forks and knives.
- To avoid last-minute cooking, or if your facilities are limited, plan one hot dish that will keep warm in a large kettle or casserole until serving time.
- Think twice about using perishable foods or sauces and gravies that separate—they can give a bad appearance.
- Keep seasons and temperature in mind when deciding on a menu (serve some cool dishes in warm weather; some hot dishes in cold weather).
- Vary the types of dishes served—but *do* make them compatible. It's likely that guests will sample almost everything.
- To make sure hot foods stay hot, use warming trays and crock pots. Or, to keep cold foods chilled, set in bowls of ice. Also, replenish dishes often rather than put out large quantities in the beginning.

PREPARATION TIPS

- Check refrigerator and freezer space. If you have to borrow freezer space from a neighbor, jot down "what dishes are where."
- Polish silver *days* ahead.
- To avoid embarrassments, like a toilet backing up or chairs collapsing, make all necessary repairs. You might assign responsibility to members of your family and include a completion date.
- If you plan to use hired help, have them arrive well before guests. Give them a quick training session, plus written instructions to follow.
- Stock up on your ice supply. *Remember:* Bagged ice from machines stays colder longer than do homemade ice cubes. Also, large blocks of ice melt more slowly; cracked ice chills drinks the quickest.
- Stack plates eight to ten high on the buffet table—it looks less institutional. Replenish as needed.
- If you have the space, set up the champagne and wedding cake away from the main buffet table. Or set up a single buffet table like this:

plates	centerpiece or wedding cake	napkins and utensils
appetizer		beverage
entrée		glasses
salad	vegetables	bread

Shrimp Newburg Tartlets*
Curried Tuna Chiffon Mold*
Nutted Rice Torta*
Ham and Cheese Paté Slices*
Broccoli Beignets*
Stuffed Turkey Breast Galantine*
Glazed Corned Beef
Crispy Breaded Vegetables
Dilled Mushrooms and Carrots*
Assortment of Rolls
Wine   Mixed Drinks   Fruit Punch
Hearts and Bells Wedding Cake*
Jordan Almonds   Party Mints
Champagne or
Champagne Blossom Punch*

*Recipe given

SHRIMP NEWBURG TARTLETS

Bake at 400° for 15 minutes, then at 300° for 15 minutes.
Makes 3 dozen tartlets.

- **1 package piecrust mix**
- **3 jars (4¼ ounces each) tiny cocktail shrimp, drained**
- **¼ cup (½ stick) butter or margarine**
- **1 tablespoon flour**
- **½ teaspoon salt**
- **¼ teaspoon pepper**
- **Dash ground nutmeg**
- **1 cup light cream or half-and-half**
- **1 egg yolk**
- **2 tablespoons dry sherry**

1. Preheat oven to 400°. Prepare piecrust mix following label directions.
2. Roll out, half at a time, ⅛-inch thick, on a lightly floured pastry board. Cut into rounds with a 2½-inch cutter; fit each into a small muffin-pan cup, pressing firmly against bottom and side. Reroll trimmings to make 36 shells in all. Prick shells well with a fork.
3. Bake in a preheated hot oven (400°) for 15 minutes or until golden. Remove carefully from pans; cool completely on wire racks. Lower oven to 300°.
4. Reserve 36 shrimp; divide remainder among the shells. Place shells in a jelly-roll pan.
5. Melt butter in a small saucepan; stir in flour, salt, pepper and nutmeg. Cook, stirring, until bubbly. Stir in cream; continue stirring until sauce thickens and bubbles 3 minutes.
6. Beat egg yolk in a small bowl; beat in half of the hot sauce, then stir back into sauce in pan. Cook, stirring 1 minute; stir in sherry. Spoon over shrimp.
7. Bake in a preheated slow oven (300°) for 15 minutes or until filling is set. Garnish with reserved shrimp. Serve hot.

CURRIED TUNA CHIFFON MOLD

Makes about 20 servings.

    1 can (13¾ ounces) chicken
       broth
    ¼ cup cold water
    2 envelopes unflavored
       gelatin
    ¾ cup chopped onion
    ¾ cup chopped celery
    2 tablespoons butter or
       margarine
    2 tablespoons curry powder
    1 can (13 ounces) tuna,
       drained
    ¼ cup chopped fresh parsley
    ½ cup finely chopped
       walnuts
    1 tablespoon lemon juice
    1 teaspoon salt
    1 cup mayonnaise

1. Combine chicken broth and water in a saucepan. Sprinkle gelatin over; let stand 5 minutes to soften. Heat mixture over very low heat, stirring until gelatin is dissolved and mixture clears; cool.
2. Sauté onion and celery in butter in a skillet until tender, about 5 minutes. Stir in curry powder; cook 1 minute.
3. Flake tuna into a large bowl, breaking up until it is very fine. Add parsley, nuts, lemon juice, salt, mayonnaise, sautéed onion and celery. Stir in cooled gelatin mixture; pour into a 5-cup ring mold. Refrigerate 4 hours or until firm.
4. Unmold onto chilled serving dish. Garnish with cherry tomatoes and cucumber slices, if you wish. Serve with crackers.

Note: May be prepared and covered with plastic wrap up to 3 days before serving. Store in refrigerator.

NUTTED RICE TORTA

Bake at 350° for 30 minutes.
Makes about 60.

    ¾ cup uncooked long-grain
       rice
    1 package (10 ounces) frozen
       chopped spinach
    5 eggs
    1 container (15 ounces) ricotta
       cheese
    1 cup grated Parmesan
       cheese
    1 teaspoon salt
    ⅛ teaspoon pepper
    2 tablespoons olive oil
    ¼ cup packaged bread crumbs
    ⅓ cup sliced almonds

1. Cook rice following label directions.

Wedding Reception Buffet: Hearts and Bells Wedding Cake, page 104

Cook spinach following label directions; drain well; squeeze out as much water as possible.
2. Beat eggs slightly in large bowl. Measure and reserve 3 tablespoons of the egg. Add rice, spinach, ricotta, Parmesan, salt and pepper to the large bowl. Stir mixture well.
3. Preheat oven to 350°. Brush bottom and sides of a 13 × 9 × 2-inch baking pan with olive oil; sprinkle with bread crumbs. Spoon in egg-cheese mixture, leveling top surface. Brush top with reserved beaten egg; sprinkle with almonds.
4. Bake in a preheated moderate oven (350°) for 30 minutes or until firm. Remove to wire rack; cut into 1¼-inch squares; transfer to warm serving platter.

Note: Baked torta may be refrigerated for up to 4 days. Reheat in moderate oven (350°) for 15 minutes. Baked torta may be frozen in pan. Cut before freezing and wrapping. Defrost in refrigerator. Reheat in moderate oven (350°) for 15 minutes.

HAM AND CHEESE PÂTÉ SLICES

Makes about 60 slices.

    10 tablespoons (1¼ sticks) butter,
       softened
    3 tablespoons Dijon mustard
    ½ teaspoon ground allspice
    ⅛ teaspoon ground nutmeg
    ¼ teaspoon freshly ground black
       pepper
    ¼ teaspoon leaf thyme,
       crumbled
    1½ pounds cooked ham
    1½ ounces Swiss cheese (in one
       piece)
    1½ ounces sharp Cheddar cheese
       (in one piece)
    1 long slender loaf French bread
    12 gherkins

1. Combine butter, mustard, allspice, nutmeg, pepper and thyme in a large bowl; mix well until smooth.
2. Grind ham, using finest disc; add to butter mixture, blending well.
3. Slice Swiss and Cheddar cheese into ¼-inch-thick sticks.
4. Turn bread top-side down; cut off ends. Make a lengthwise cut down the center of the loaf from one end to the other, being careful not to cut through top side. Spread the bread apart carefully; hollow it out, leaving about ½-inch-thick shell. (The bread removed from the center can be dried and used for bread crumbs.)
5. Press half the ham mixture into the bread. Arrange the Swiss cheese sticks

lengthwise in one row; arrange the gherkins as the center row, the Cheddar as the third row. Press the remaining ham mixture on top. Close up the two halves of the bread. Wrap tightly in plastic wrap; then in foil. Refrigerate for several hours or overnight.
6. To serve: Slice filled loaf thinly; arrange slices, overlapping, on serving tray.

Note: Pâté loaf may be kept wrapped and refrigerated for up to 3 days before serving.

BROCCOLI BEIGNETS

Makes 36.

    ½ small bunch broccoli
    ½ cup (1 stick) butter or
       margarine
    1 cup water
    1 teaspoon salt
       Pinch garlic powder
    1 cup *sifted* all-purpose flour
    4 eggs
       Vegetable oil for frying
    ½ cup grated Parmesan cheese

1. Trim broccoli; pare stems. Cut flowerets into 1-inch pieces and stems into ¼-inch slices. (You should have about 2 cups.) Cook, covered, in boiling water in a large saucepan for 5 minutes; drain; mash or chop finely.
2. Combine butter, water, salt and garlic powder in a large saucepan. Heat until water is boiling and butter is melted. Add flour all at once; remove from heat. Stir mixture quickly with a wooden spoon until dough comes away from side of pan and forms mound in center.
3. Add eggs, 1 at a time, beating well after each addition until mixture is smooth. Stir broccoli into dough; chill 2 hours or overnight.
4. Pour enough oil into a deep skillet or large saucepan to make a 3-inch depth. Heat to 375° on a deep-fat frying thermometer or until hot enough that a bit of the mixture will sizzle and pop to the surface when dropped into the oil.
5. Scoop up a heaping teaspoonful of the dough and push it off into the oil with another teaspoon. Continue with spoonsful of dough, frying just a small batch at a time, so pan is not crowded. Brown beignets on one side about 2 minutes, then turn and brown on other. Remove puffed browned beignets with a slotted spoon to paper toweling to drain. Sprinkle with Parmesan cheese and serve piping hot.

Note: Dough may be prepared the day before. Beignets may be fried several hours before serving. Heat on a cookie sheet in a moderate oven (350°) for 10 minutes.

STUFFED TURKEY BREAST GALANTINE

Makes 10 servings.

- **¼ pound chicken livers**
- **¼ cup (½ stick) butter or margarine**
- **¼ pound mushrooms, finely chopped**
- **½ cup chopped green onions**
- **¼ cup chopped fresh parsley**
- **1 cup fresh bread crumbs, slightly dried (2 slices)**
- **4 teaspoons salt**
- **¼ teaspoon ground pepper**
- **1 egg**
- **1 whole turkey breast (about 6½ pounds), thawed if frozen**
- **5 cups water**
- **1 carrot, quartered**
- **1 onion, halved**
- **½ teaspoon leaf thyme, crumbled**
- **1 bay leaf**
- **Chaud-Froid Glaze (recipe follows)**
- **Tomato peel, lemon peel, green onion tops (for garnish)**
- **Watercress**

1. Sauté chicken livers in butter in a small skillet just until firm; remove with slotted spoon to wooden board and chop finely. Add mushrooms to remaining butter in same skillet; sauté until tender, stirring about 5 minutes. Add onions; sauté 2 minutes. Remove to a bowl; add chicken livers, parsley, crumbs, 1 teaspoon of the salt, pepper and egg.
2. Place turkey breast, skin-side down, on board. With a sharp, thin-bladed knife, carefully remove breastbone from meat without piercing skin. Spoon dressing onto center of boned breast. Press meat around stuffing; fasten with skewers, then wrap tightly in cheesecloth. Tie with string.
3. Place rolled turkey and the bones in Dutch oven or large kettle. Add water, carrot, onion, remaining salt, thyme and bay leaf. Bring to boiling; lower heat; cover. Simmer, turning once, about 2 hours. Cool in broth for 1 hour.
4. Remove turkey roll from broth; unwrap from cheesecloth. Place in shallow dish; cover; refrigerate overnight. Strain broth; refrigerate.
5. Several hours or the day before serving, glaze and decorate: Place cold turkey roll on cookie sheet or jelly-roll pan, skin-side up. Spoon Chaud-Froid Glaze over several times until heavily and evenly coated. Chill between each coating. Arrange on serving platter. Deco-rate with tomato and lemon peels cut into flower petals. Use green onion tops for stems. Garnish with watercress.

Chaud-Froid Glaze: Boil 1½ cups of reserved broth and ⅛ teaspoon leaf tarragon until reduced to 1 cup; stir in 1 envelope gelatin, softened in ¼ cup cold water, until dissolved. Add ¾ cup heavy cream and strain into a small bowl. Chill until syrupy.

DILLED MUSHROOMS AND CARROTS

Makes about 12 cups.

- **3 pounds small fresh mushrooms**
- **1 pound carrots, pared and cut into 1-inch chunks**
- **4 tablespoons salt**
- **2 cups water**
- **2 cups distilled white vinegar**
- **¼ cup dillweed**
- **½ cup sugar**
- **1½ teaspoons peppercorns**

1. Cook mushrooms and carrots in boiling water to cover in a kettle for 5 minutes. Drain well. Place in a large glass bowl.
2. Combine salt, water, vinegar, dillweed, sugar and peppercorns in saucepan. Bring to boiling; pour over vegetables. Cover and refrigerate. Drain before serving.

EASY GARNISHES TO DRESS UP YOUR FOOD

Onion Mum: Cut off stem end of 1 medium-size round onion; peel, leaving root on. Cut thin vertical slices from top to root end, but not through the root. Give the onion a quarter turn; repeat slicing. Soak onion mum in ice water for 2 hours or more. Slices will open like a flower. Place on greens to garnish platter.

Radish Roses: Trim large long radish. Cut 5 or 6 petals with a sharp paring knife by starting cut near the top of the radish and cutting a thin paring of the red skin down toward the root end. Do not cut through. Remove white radish core, forming a hollow flower with red petals. Soak in ice water for at least 2 hours. Petals will open out. Cut a pimiento-stuffed olive in half, crosswise; fasten to center of radish.

Grapefruit Roses: Remove the yellow skin of 3 thick-skinned grapefruits with a vegetable parer, leaving the white. Pare the white with a paring knife, down to the flesh of the grapefruit in an unbroken spiral paring. Roll the white back into its natural spiral shape (the stem end forms the base of the spiral); fasten with wooden picks.

Combine a 1-ounce bottle of red food coloring with ½ cup water in a small bowl. Immerse the roses, turning with a spoon, until they have turned completely red. Remove and drain. Place on greens to decorate platter.

HEARTS AND BELLS WEDDING CAKE

The base is a brandied pound cake and it is topped with a fruited pound cake, a small tier that can be saved for the bride and groom's first anniversary.

Bake at 325° for 1½ hours.
Makes about 30 servings.

- **5 cups *sifted* cake flour**
- **3 teaspoons baking powder**
- **1 teaspoon salt**
- **1½ cups (3 sticks) butter or margarine**
- **2¼ cups sugar**
- **6 eggs**
- **¾ cup apricot nectar**
- **¼ cup brandy or sherry**
- **2 cups (1 pound) mixed candied fruits**
- **1 can (3½ ounces) sliced almonds**
- **Sugar Wedding Bells (recipe follows)**
- **Almond Butter Frosting (recipe follows)**
- **Royal Frosting (recipe follows)**

1. Grease and lightly flour one 10 × 3-inch pan and one 7-inch or 8 × 2-inch spring-form pan with loose bottom.
2. Sift flour, baking powder and salt onto wax paper.
3. Preheat oven to 325°. Beat butter in large bowl with electric mixer until soft; gradually add sugar and continue beating until mixture is well blended. Beat in eggs, 1 at a time, until mixture is light and fluffy.
4. Combine apricot nectar and brandy. Stir flour mixture into batter with spoon, alternately with apricot-brandy mixture, beating well after each addition until batter is smooth. Mix about 2 cups of batter with candied fruits and almonds; pour into 7-inch pan. Pour remaining batter into 10-inch pan. Spread tops smooth.
5. Bake in a preheated slow oven (325°) for 1½ hours or until tops spring back when lightly pressed with fingertip. Cool in pans on wire racks 10 minutes. Loosen around edges with a small spatula; loosen and remove from bottom; cool completely. Wrap cakes and refrigerate or freeze until ready to frost and deco-

rate. Cakes can be refrigerated up to 3 days or frozen for up to 2 weeks.

6. Prepare Sugar Wedding Bells the day before the cake is to be decorated; let dry overnight.

7. Prepare Almond Butter Frosting.

8. Place large cake on serving plate or tray. Frost side and top with part of Almond Butter Frosting. Center small cake on top; frost. Outline hearts with a wooden pick, spacing evenly around sides of both layers.

9. Prepare Royal Frosting. Fit pastry bag or tube of cake decorating set with a small star tip. Pipe frosting around heart outlines and around cake tiers.

10. Pipe a small mound of Royal Frosting on the top tier and in evenly spaced areas on bottom tier. Press Sugar Wedding Bells into frosting. Add bows of narrow satin ribbon and tiny nosegays of fresh flowers, if you wish.

11. To cut: Slice bottom tier first; lift off top tier and save or serve. Cut center of bottom tier last.

Sugar Wedding Bells: Mix 4 to 5 teaspoons cold water with sugar until moistened enough to pack into a ball. Pack sugar into a small bell-shaped egg cup or cordial glass to fill; unmold immediately onto wax paper. Allow to dry 2 to 3 hours; carefully hollow out with a small knife to make a shell 1/8- to 1/4-inch thick. Let bells dry overnight. (Reshape the scooped-out sugar to make more bells.) Pipe a decorative edge with Royal Frosting. Allow to dry. Makes about 10 bells.

Almond Butter Frosting: Beat 10 tablespoons butter or margarine and half an 8-ounce can almond paste together in medium-size bowl with electric mixer until very smooth; beat in 3 1/2 cups 10X sugar alternately with 3 to 4 tablespoons milk until smooth. Makes about 3 1/4 cups.

Royal Frosting: Beat 2 egg whites and 1/4 teaspoon cream of tartar together in small bowl until foamy. Gradually beat in 2 1/2 to 3 cups 10X sugar until frosting stands in firm peaks and holds its shape when cut with a knife. (Keep bowl covered with damp paper toweling while working to keep frosting from drying out.) Makes about 2 cups.

Overleaf: Frosty Christmas Tree Cookies, page 108; (center) Almond Crescents, page 108; (far left) Raspberry-Almond Cookies, page 110; Chocolate-Nut Tassies, page 108; Lebkuchen, page 109; (right) Cookie Pretzels, page 109; Noel Wreaths, page 109

HOW TO MAKE DECORATIVE EDGINGS

Work out the designs on the frosting with a wooden pick. Then it is simple to follow the design with the pastry bag.

Shell Border: Fit the #98 Shell Tip onto the pastry bag. Press out frosting in overlapping shell design around entire top edge of tier (see Fig. 1).

String Scallops: Fit the #2 Writing Tip onto the pastry bag. Mark out scallop pattern in a double scallop. Press out the frosting, following design, making single scallop all the way around. Follow with second scallop row to make double scalloping (see Fig. 2).

Diamond Pattern: Using same #2 Writing Tip, mark out diamond pattern on third tier with wooden pick. Press all lines in one direction first, then follow with crisscross lines to complete pattern.

Drop Flowers: Fit the #96 Drop-Flower Tip or #27 Star Tip onto pastry bag. Holding the tip about 1/16-inch away from the cake, squeeze, relax pressure, then pull tip away. Continue all around (see Fig. 3).

Fluted Scallops: Fit the #27 Star Tip onto pastry bag. Mark out scallop pattern on top tier with wooden pick. Follow pattern, pressing out the frosting all around tier.

Leaves: Fit the #67 Leaf Tip onto pastry bag. Press out frosting with a backward and forward motion, then break off pressure with a quick motion to make pointed tip of leaf (see Fig. 4).

CHAMPAGNE BLOSSOM PUNCH

Makes 100 three-ounce servings.

- **1 can (12 ounces) frozen orange juice concentrate, thawed**
- **1 can (12 ounces) frozen lemonade concentrate, thawed**
- **1 gallon sauterne or Riesling wine, chilled**
- **6 bottles (750 ml. each) champagne, chilled**
- **Rosebuds *(optional)***

1. Combine frozen concentrates in large bowl; gradually add wine and stir until completely dissolved. Chill until serving time.

2. Just before serving, transfer mixture to large punch bowl; add ice cubes, then champagne. Garnish with orange and lime slices or float a few well-washed rosebuds on punch.

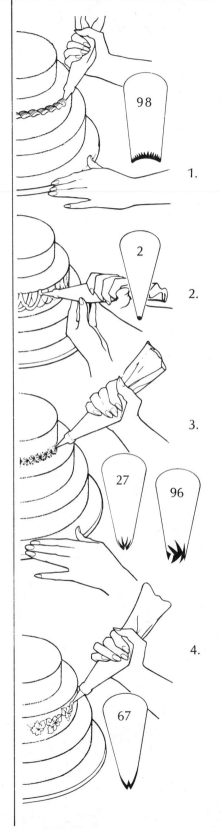

1.
2.
3.
27 96
4.
67

COOKIES FOR SPECIAL OCCASIONS

Bake a batch of cookies for your child's birthday party, for a school social or to sell at a church bazaar. And of course it wouldn't be Christmas without cookie-baking. We have put together this delicious batch of all-time favorites, some with a new twist. There's something here for every special occasion.

FROSTY CHRISTMAS TREE COOKIES

Crispy molasses cookie trees sparkle with sugar frosting.

Bake at 350° for 8 minutes.
Makes 3 dozen cookies.

    3¾ cups *sifted* all-purpose flour
    1 teaspoon baking soda
    ½ teaspoon salt
    2 tablespoons unsweetened
      cocoa powder
    2 teaspoons ground ginger
    3 teaspoons ground cinnamon
    2 teaspoons ground cloves
    1 cup (2 sticks) butter, softened
    1 cup sugar
    1 egg
    ½ cup molasses
      Sugar Icing *(recipe follows)*
      Colored decorating sugar

1. Sift flour, baking soda, salt, cocoa, ginger, cinnamon and cloves onto wax paper.
2. Beat butter, sugar, egg and molasses in a large bowl with electric mixer until fluffy-light. Stir in flour mixture until well blended. Wrap dough in plastic wrap or foil; refrigerate several hours or overnight.
3. Preheat oven to 350°. Roll out dough, ⅓ at a time, on a lightly floured surface to a ¼-inch thickness. Cut out with floured large Christmas tree cutter. Brush off excess flour; place cookies on lightly greased cookie sheets. Repeat with remaining dough. Gather up scraps for second rolling.
4. Bake in a preheated moderate oven (350°) for 8 minutes or until edges are browned. Let cookies cool a few minutes on cookie sheets. Remove to wire racks with a spatula; cool completely. Dip small clean brush into Sugar Icing and "paint" cookies. Sprinkle with colored sugars.

Sugar Icing: Combine 1 package (1 pound) 10X (confectioners') sugar, 1 teaspoon vanilla and ⅓ cup water in a medium-size bowl; stir until smooth. Add more water, a teaspoon at a time, until icing is spoonable and flows easily. Makes about 2 cups.

APRICOT PINWHEELS

A lightly spiced sugar cookie with a swirl of tangy apricot.

Bake at 350° for 10 minutes.
Makes 8 dozen cookies.

    1 cup chopped dried apricots
    ¾ cup water
    ½ cup sugar
    1 cup finely chopped pecans
    3½ cups *sifted* all-purpose flour
    ½ teaspoon salt
    ½ teaspoon baking soda
    ¼ teaspoon ground nutmeg
    ⅛ teaspoon ground cloves
    1 cup vegetable shortening
    2 cups firmly packed light brown
      sugar
    2 eggs
      Vanilla Butter Frosting *(recipe
      follows)*

1. Combine apricots, water and sugar in a small saucepan. Bring to boiling; lower heat; simmer 10 minutes. Remove from heat; puree in container of electric blender. Cool; stir in nuts.
2. Sift flour, salt, baking soda, nutmeg and cloves onto wax paper.
3. Beat shortening, sugar and eggs in large bowl with electric mixer until fluffy-light. Stir in flour mixture until well blended. Wrap in plastic wrap or foil; refrigerate 2 hours or overnight.
4. Divide chilled dough in half. Roll out between sheets of lightly floured wax paper to a 13 × 9-inch rectangle. (Moisten counter top with water to hold bottom sheet in place.) Lift onto a cookie sheet; place in refrigerator for 30 minutes.
5. Remove top sheet of wax paper. Spread dough with half the apricot filling to within ¼-inch of the edges. Roll dough, jelly-roll style, from one of the long sides, lifting up dough with bottom sheet of wax paper to start rolling. Wrap roll in plastic wrap or foil; chill several hours or overnight. Repeat with remaining half of dough and filling.
6. Preheat oven to 350°. Cut chilled dough in ¼-inch-thick slices. Place 2 inches apart on lightly greased cookie sheets.
7. Bake in a moderate oven (350°) for 10 minutes or until lightly browned. Cool on wire racks.
8. Spoon Vanilla Butter Frosting into a pastry bag or cake decorator fitted with a small round tip. Pipe onto cookies following the spiral shape.

Vanilla Butter Frosting: Beat ¼ cup (½ stick) softened butter, ½ teaspoon vanilla and 1 cup *sifted* 10X (confectioners') sugar in a medium-size bowl until smooth. Add 1 to 2 teaspoons of milk if mixture is too stiff to pipe. Makes 2 cups.

ALMOND CRESCENTS

These nutted little gems literally melt in your mouth.

Bake at 350° for 15 minutes.
Makes 4 dozen cookies.

    2 cups *sifted* all-purpose flour
    ¼ teaspoon salt
    1 cup (2 sticks) unsalted butter,
      softened
    ¼ cup sugar
    ½ teaspoon almond extract
    1 cup whole blanched almonds
      (about 4½ ounces), finely
      ground
    10X (confectioners') sugar
    3 squares semisweet chocolate
    1 tablespoon butter

1. Sift flour and salt onto wax paper.
2. Beat the 1 cup butter, sugar and almond extract in a medium-size bowl until smooth. Stir in flour until well blended. Stir in almonds. Wrap dough in plastic wrap or foil; refrigerate several hours or overnight.
3. Preheat oven to 350°. Roll dough, a heaping teaspoonful at a time, into 1-inch balls. Roll each ball with palms of hands on a lightly floured surface to a 3-inch length. Form into a crescent shape and place 2 inches apart on lightly greased cookie sheets.
4. Bake in a preheated moderate oven (350°) for 15 minutes. Remove from oven; cool slightly; transfer to wire racks. Sift 10X sugar through a fine sieve over the warm cookies or roll in 10X sugar, tapping off excess.
5. Melt chocolate and 1 tablespoon butter over hot, not boiling, water. Drizzle mixture over cookies with a small spoon. Store cookies in a tightly covered container with wax paper between layers.

CHOCOLATE-NUT TASSIES

A tiny cookie cup filled with luscious fruit jam and topped with chocolate.

Bake at 350° for 13 minutes.
Makes 2 dozen cookies.

    ½ cup (1 stick) butter,
      softened
    1 package (3 ounces) cream
      cheese, softened
    3 tablespoons sugar
    ½ teaspoon vanilla
    1 cup *sifted* all-purpose flour
    ¼ cup finely ground blanched
      almonds
    ¼ cup raspberry, strawberry or
      apricot jam
    2 squares semisweet chocolate
    1 tablespoon butter
    1 tube red icing
    1 tube green icing

1. Beat butter, cream cheese, sugar and vanilla in a medium-size bowl until fluffy-light. Stir in flour until smooth. Stir in nuts until well blended. Wrap dough in plastic wrap or foil; refrigerate several hours or overnight.
2. Preheat oven to 350°. Divide dough into 24 equal-size pieces. Gently press each piece into bottom and up the side of an ungreased 1¾-inch muffin-pan cup to form a shell.
3. Bake in a preheated moderate oven (350°) for 13 minutes or until lightly browned. Remove from oven to wire racks; cool slightly. Gently loosen cookies with tip of a paring knife; lift out of pans; cool completely.
4. When cookie shells are cool, spoon about ½ teaspoon of jam into each, leaving about ⅛ inch of space at the top.
5. Melt chocolate and butter over hot, not boiling, water; cool slightly. Spoon a layer of the chocolate mixture over the jam layer. Refrigerate until chocolate sets, about 1 hour. Decorate with Christmas motifs using tube icing. Keep refrigerated.

COOKIE PRETZELS

You have a choice of frostings for these almond-scented little delicacies.

Bake at 350° for 10 minutes.
Makes 4½ dozen cookies.

> **1 cup (2 sticks) butter, softened**
> **⅔ cup sugar**
> **3 egg yolks**
> **1 teaspoon almond extract**
> **2⅓ cups** *sifted* **all-purpose flour**
> **Vanilla Icing** *(recipe follows)*
> **Chocolate Icing** *(recipe follows)*
> **Multi-colored sprinkles**
> **Silver dragees**

1. Beat butter, sugar, egg yolks and almond extract in a medium-size bowl with an electric mixer until fluffy-light. Stir in flour, blending well. Wrap dough in plastic wrap or foil; refrigerate overnight.
2. Preheat oven to 350°. Roll dough, 1 teaspoonful at a time, into balls slightly less than 1 inch. Roll each ball with palms of hands on a lightly floured surface to a 9-inch length. Pick up one end in each hand, cross over, fold back onto the circle and press down, forming pretzel shape. Gently transfer each pretzel to an ungreased cookie sheet with a spatula, spacing 2 inches apart.
3. Bake in a preheated moderate oven (350°) for 10 minutes or until firm (cookies will be pale). Remove from oven; cool slightly; transfer to a wire rack.

4. When thoroughly cooled, dip cookies, top-side down, into Vanilla or Chocolate Icing. Remove with a fork and place, right-side up, on wire rack placed over wax paper, to catch drips. Before icing sets, sprinkle with multi-colored sprinkles or dragees.

Vanilla Icing: Combine 3 egg whites, lightly beaten, 3¾ cups *sifted* 10X (confectioners') sugar and 1 teaspoon vanilla in a medium-size bowl. Beat with electric mixer until smooth. Makes about 1⅓ cups.

Chocolate Icing: Combine 3 egg whites, lightly beaten, 2¾ cups *sifted* 10X (confectioners') sugar and 3 tablespoons unsweetened cocoa powder in a medium-size bowl. Beat with electric mixer until smooth. Makes about 1¼ cups.

LEBKUCHEN

Store these spicy, fruited morsels a week or so to mellow and soften.

Bake at 350° for 12 minutes for small cookies, and 15 minutes for large cookies.
Makes 12 large cookies or 24 small cookies.

> **¾ cup honey**
> **¾ cup firmly packed dark brown sugar**
> **1 egg**
> **2 teaspoons grated lemon rind**
> **3 tablespoons lemon juice**
> **3½ cups** *sifted* **all-purpose flour**
> **1 teaspoon salt**
> **1 teaspoon ground cinnamon**
> **1 teaspoon ground nutmeg**
> **½ teaspoon ground allspice**
> **½ teaspoon ground ginger**
> **¼ teaspoon ground cloves**
> **½ teaspoon baking soda**
> **1 container (8 ounces) candied orange peel, chopped**
> **1 cup chopped unblanched almonds**
> **Sugar Glaze** *(recipe follows)*
> **Pecan halves**
> **Candied red cherries**

1. Heat honey to boiling in a small saucepan; pour into a large bowl; cool about 30 minutes.
2. Stir brown sugar, egg, lemon rind and lemon juice into cooled honey, blending well.
3. Sift flour, salt, cinnamon, nutmeg, allspice, ginger, cloves and baking soda onto wax paper. Stir into honey mixture, a third at a time, until well blended. Stir in candied orange peel and almonds. Dough will be stiff, but sticky. Wrap in plastic wrap or foil; refrigerate several hours or overnight.
4. Preheat oven to 350°. Roll out ¼ of the dough on a lightly floured surface to a 9 × 7-inch rectangle. (Keep remaining dough refrigerated.) Even sides of

dough, then cut crosswise into 3 equal strips, each about 7 × 3 inches (for large cookies). OR: Cut the same way, but cut each rectangle in half to make two 3½ × 3-inch rectangles (for small cookies). Repeat with remaining chilled dough, working with ¼ at a time. Place cookies 1 inch apart on greased cookie sheets.
5. Bake in a preheated moderate oven (350°) for about 12 minutes for the small cookies and 15 minutes for the large cookies or until firm. Remove cookies to wire racks. Brush hot cookies with hot Sugar Glaze. Decorate small cookies with pecans and candied red cherries. Decorate the large cookies with Santa Claus cutouts using a "glue" of 10X sugar and water. Store cookies in a tightly covered container with wax paper between layers for a week or two to mellow.

Sugar Glaze: Combine ¾ cup granulated sugar and ⅓ cup water in a small saucepan. Bring to boiling, stirring constantly; lower heat; simmer 3 minutes. Remove from heat; stir in ¼ cup 10X (confectioners') sugar. Makes about ¾ cup.

NOEL WREATHS

Buttery little wreaths with fruited centers.
Bake at 350° for 12 minutes.
Makes 4 dozen cookies.

> **1 cup (2 sticks) butter, softened**
> **½ cup sugar**
> **1 egg**
> **1 teaspoon vanilla**
> **2½ cups** *sifted* **all-purpose flour**
> **1 cup finely chopped walnuts**
> **¼ cup finely chopped raisins**
> **¼ cup honey**
> **Candied red and green cherries**

1. Beat butter, sugar, egg and vanilla in a medium-size bowl with electric mixer until fluffy-light. Stir in flour gradually to make a soft dough.
2. Measure out ⅓ cup of the dough; transfer to a small bowl. Blend in walnuts, raisins and honey; reserve.
3. Preheat oven to 350°. Spoon remaining dough into a pastry bag fitted with a small star tip. Press out into 1½-inch rings on ungreased large cookie sheets. Fill center of each cookie with about a teaspoonful of the reserved nut mixture. Decorate wreaths with slivers of cherries.
4. Bake in a preheated moderate oven (350°) for 12 minutes or until lightly golden at edges. Remove from cookie sheets to wire racks; cool completely. Store in tightly covered containers.

RASPBERRY-ALMOND COOKIES

Almond cookies sandwiched with tart raspberry jam.

Bake at 350° for 8 minutes.
Makes 1½ dozen cookies.

- **1 cup (2 sticks) butter, softened**
- **½ cup granulated sugar**
- **1 egg**
- **½ cup almond paste (not almond filling or marzipan)**
- **2¼ cups *sifted* all-purpose flour**
- **1 teaspoon grated lemon rind**
- **10X (confectioners') sugar**
- **1 cup red raspberry jam, sieved**
- **Whole blanched almonds**

1. Beat butter, sugar and egg in a large bowl with electric mixer until smooth. Crumble in almond paste; beat until well blended.
2. Gradually add flour, blending thoroughly; stir in lemon rind. Wrap dough in plastic wrap or foil (mixture will be sticky). Refrigerate several hours or overnight.
3. Preheat oven to 350°. Divide chilled dough in half. Roll out between sheets of lightly floured wax paper to an ⅛-inch thickness. (Moisten countertop with water to hold bottom sheet in place.) Chill briefly if too soft. Cut out with a 4-inch floured star-shaped cutter. Place 1 inch apart on an ungreased cookie sheet. Refrigerate scraps for a second rolling.
4. Roll out remaining half of dough. Cut out star shapes. Cut out centers of stars with a ½-inch round cutter. Save scraps for second rolling. (Be sure you have enough solid cookies to match the cut-out cookies.) Reroll the scraps cutting equal number of solids and cutouts.
5. Bake in a preheated moderate oven (350°) for 8 minutes or until edges of cookies are lightly browned. Remove from oven; let stand 1 minute. Remove to wire racks; cool thoroughly.
6. Sift 10X sugar through a fine strainer over the cut-out cookies. Spread the solid cookies with a thin layer of jam. Press together to make a sandwich. Add a bit more jam in the center; top with a whole almond.

ALMOND SPRITZ COOKIES

Bake at 400° for 7 minutes.
Makes about 5 dozen cookies.

- **1 cup (2 sticks) butter, softened**
- **⅔ cup sugar**
- **3 egg yolks**
- **1 teaspoon vanilla**
- **2½ cups *sifted* all-purpose flour**
- **1 egg white**
- **1 cup sliced almonds**

1. Preheat oven to 400°. Beat butter, sugar, egg yolks and vanilla in a medium-size bowl until well blended. Blend in flour gradually until soft dough forms.
2. Using a cookie press or a pastry bag fitted with a large plain tip, pipe cookie dough out onto ungreased cookie sheets. Brush unbaked cookie dough with slightly beaten egg white; press sliced almonds into dough.
3. Bake in a preheated hot oven (400°) for 7 minutes or until golden brown. Remove to wire racks; cool.

Chocolate Dipped: Shape, bake and cool cookies. Melt 1 package (6 ounces) semi-sweet chocolate pieces and 1 teaspoon vegetable shortening in top of double boiler over hot, not boiling, water; cool. Dip ends of cookies into chocolate, then into finely chopped walnuts. Let stand until firm.

RUM-BUTTER FROSTED BROWNIES

Bake at 350° for 30 minutes.
Makes about 30 one-inch bars.

- **4 squares unsweetened chocolate**
- **1 cup (2 sticks) butter**
- **4 eggs**
- **2 cups sugar**
- **2 teaspoons vanilla**
- **1 cup *sifted* all-purpose flour**
- **¼ teaspoon salt**
- **1½ cups chopped walnuts**
- **Rum Butter Cream (recipe follows)**
- **4 squares unsweetened chocolate**

1. Melt 4 squares chocolate and butter in a saucepan over low heat; cool.
2. Preheat oven to 350°. Beat eggs in a medium-size bowl with electric mixer until fluffy. Gradually beat in sugar until mixture is thick. Stir in chocolate mixture and vanilla. Fold in flour and salt until well blended. Stir in walnuts. Spread evenly in a well-greased 13 × 9 × 2-inch baking pan.
3. Bake in a moderate oven (350°) for 30 minutes or until shiny and firm on top. Cool completely in pan on wire rack.
4. Spread cooled brownies with Rum Butter Cream.
5. Melt remaining chocolate in small saucepan over very low heat; cool. Spread evenly over Rum Butter Cream. Let stand until firm. Cut into bars.

Rum Butter Cream: Blend ½ cup (1 stick) softened butter with half a 1-pound box 10X (confectioners') sugar in a medium-size bowl. Beat in remaining sugar alternately with 3 to 4 tablespoons golden rum until frosting is of good spreading consistency.

JOB PROMOTION

Honor a friend or family member who has been promoted with a cheese, fruit and wine party. Because people will be driving home or departing for dinner later, you shouldn't serve too much food or drinks. The tradition of serving cocktails with canapés is giving way these days to a wider range of lighter wine-based drinks. Wine, plain or on the rocks as a spritzer, is light on the diet and pocketbook. For the health-conscious guests who have deserted alcoholic drinks, serve sparkling or still mineral water, fruit juice or soft drinks. When selecting cheeses for the party, choose any variety except the hard-grating ones and soft, unripened cheeses like ricotta. Choose at least three types of cheese with different flavors, textures, colors and shapes. Purchase at least 4 ounces of cheese per person but buy more of a hard cheese for the sake of appearance because hard cheeses are smaller in size to weight than soft cheeses. Remove cheese from the refrigerator an hour before serving to improve flavor.

CHEESE-WINE-FRUIT PARTY
Herbed Cheese Spread*
Blue Cheese Logs*
Sesame Seed Crackers*
Cheddar Cheese Ripples*
Fresh Fruit
Poppy Seed-Onion Crackers*
Chile con Queso*
Cumin Chips*
Wine

*Recipe given

HERBED CHEESE SPREAD

Makes 1¼ cups.

- **1 container (8 ounces) cottage cheese**
- **1 package (3 ounces) cream cheese, softened**
- **1 tablespoon chopped fresh parsley**
- **1 tablespoon chopped chives**
- **¼ teaspoon salt**
- **¼ teaspoon leaf thyme, crumbled**
- **¼ teaspoon leaf basil, crumbled**
- **¼ teaspoon leaf savory, crumbled**

Press cottage cheese through a food mill or large strainer into a medium-size bowl. Beat in cream cheese until smooth. Stir in parsley, chives, salt, thyme, basil and savory. Spoon into serving dish; cover. Refrigerate several hours.

Cheese-Wine-Fruit Party: (Foreground left) Chile con Queso, page 112; Cumin Chips, page 112; Herbed Cheese Spread, page 110; Poppy Seed-Onion Crackers; page 112; Blue Cheese Logs, page 112; Cheddar Cheese Ripples, page 112.

BLUE CHEESE LOGS

Blue cheese teams with butter and Cheddar for a zesty spread.

Makes 2 logs.

- **6 ounces blue cheese, crumbled**
- **½ cup (1 stick) butter, softened**
- **1 stick (10 ounces) extra sharp Cheddar cheese, shredded**
- **2 tablespoons brandy**
- **1 teaspoon Worcestershire sauce**
- **⅔ cup chopped walnuts**
- **⅔ cup chopped fresh parsley**

1. Beat blue cheese and butter until light and fluffy in large bowl with electric mixer. Stir in Cheddar, brandy and Worcestershire.
2. Divide mixture in half. Turn each half onto wax paper and roll, shaping into a log 1 inch in diameter. Twist ends of wax paper closed. Refrigerate several hours until firm.
3. Combine nuts and parsley. Roll cheese logs in mixture, pressing firmly. Roll up in wax paper; refrigerate. Soften slightly before serving.

SESAME SEED CRACKERS

Bake at 425° for 12 minutes.
Makes about 9 dozen.

- **2 jars (2⅝ ounces each) sesame seeds**
- **3½ cups *sifted* unbleached all-purpose flour**
- **1½ teaspoons salt**
- **¼ teaspoon chili powder**
- **1 cup (2 sticks) butter or margarine**
- **½ cup ice water**

1. Toast sesame seeds in a large skillet over low heat, stirring occasionally, until seeds are light brown. Turn into a large bowl; cool.
2. Stir in flour, salt and chili powder. Cut in butter with pastry blender until mixture is crumbly.
3. Stir in water slowly, mixing lightly with a fork just until pastry is thoroughly moistened. Gather dough·into a ball. Cover. Chill 30 minutes.
4. Preheat oven to 425°. Lightly dust two 17 × 14-inch cookie sheets with flour. Divide dough in half. Roll each half out directly on cookie sheets, covering entire sheet evenly. Patch if necessary. With pastry cutter or sharp knife, cut into 2-inch squares. Prick each square a few times with fork.
5. Bake in a preheated hot oven (425°) for 12 minutes or just until lightly browned. Remove from cookie sheets to wire racks to cool completely. Store in tightly covered containers.

CHEDDAR CHEESE RIPPLES

Bake at 350° for 15 minutes.
Makes about 7 dozen.

- **¾ cup (1½ sticks) butter or margarine, softened**
- **1 package (8 ounces) cream cheese, softened**
- **1 egg**
- **1 teaspoon salt**
- **¼ teaspoon crushed red pepper**
- **1 stick (10 ounces) extra-sharp Cheddar cheese, finely shredded**
- **2 cups *sifted* all-purpose flour**
- **1 cup ground pecans**

1. Beat butter with cream cheese in a large bowl with electric mixer. Add egg, salt and red pepper, beating until thoroughly combined. Stir in Cheddar cheese.
2. Work in flour and pecans, ⅓ at a time, with wooden spoon. Gather dough into a ball. Refrigerate 30 minutes.
3. Preheat oven to 350°. Fill cookie gun. Using saw-toothed disk, hold gun at a 45° angle and squeeze down length of large ungreased cookie sheet 1 inch apart. Cut into 3-inch lengths, leaving pieces in place.
4. Bake in a preheated moderate oven (350°) for 15 minutes or until crackers are lightly browned at edges. Remove from cookie sheets to wire racks to cool completely. Store in tightly covered containers.

POPPY SEED-ONION CRACKERS

Bake at 350° for 15 minutes.
Makes about 5½ dozen.

- **2 cups *sifted* unbleached all-purpose flour**
- **1 teaspoon baking powder**
- **1 teaspoon sugar**
- **1 teaspoon salt**
- **⅛ teaspoon white pepper**
- **⅓ cup poppy seeds**
- **1 tablespoon instant minced onion**
- **¼ cup warm water**
- **2 eggs, slightly beaten**
- **6 tablespoons vegetable oil**

1. Sift flour, baking powder, sugar, salt and pepper into a large bowl; stir in poppy seeds.
2. Preheat oven to 350°. Combine onion with water; let stand 5 minutes; drain thoroughly.
3. Add onion, eggs and oil to flour mixture; mix thoroughly with fork until moistened. Gather dough into a ball.
4. Roll out to ⅛-inch thickness on a floured surface. Cut with 1½-inch bridge cutters or a round cutter. Place 2 inches apart on ungreased cookie sheets.

5. Bake in a preheated moderate oven (350°) for 15 minutes or until edges of crackers are a light brown. Remove from cookie sheets to wire racks to cool. Store in tightly covered containers.

CHILE CON QUESO

Makes 3 cups.

- **1 medium-size onion, finely chopped (½ cup)**
- **3 tablespoons butter**
- **3 tablespoons flour**
- **1 teaspoon salt**
- **1 cup heavy cream**
- **1 can (16 ounces) tomatoes, drained and coarsely chopped**
- **1 can (4 ounces) diced mild green chilies, drained**
- **1 package (8 ounces) Monterey Jack cheese, cubed**

1. Sauté onion in butter in a medium-size saucepan until tender. Stir in flour and salt; cook, stirring constantly, just until bubbly. Remove from heat. Stir in heavy cream slowly. Return to heat and continue cooking and stirring until sauce thickens and begins to bubble, about 3 minutes.
2. Stir in tomatoes and chilies; cook 1 minute. Add cheese, stirring constantly, until melted. Serve warm.

CUMIN CHIPS

Makes about 10 dozen.

- **3 cups instant corn masa***
- **1 teaspoon salt**
- **½ teaspoon cumin seeds, crushed**
- **1½ cups water**
- **Vegetable oil for frying**
- **Salt**

1. Combine instant corn masa, salt and cumin seeds in a large bowl. Make a well in the center. Add water and mix thoroughly with fork. Gather dough into a ball. Cut into 16 equal pieces.
2. Roll out each piece between two sheets of wax paper to a 5-inch round. Keep covered with wax paper until ready to fry. Remove paper and cut rolled dough into 8 equal triangles.
3. Heat 1 inch of vegetable oil in a large skillet to 375° on a deep-fat frying thermometer.
4. Fry cumin chips, a layer at a time, until brown and crisp, turning once. Remove to paper toweling to drain. Sprinkle lightly with salt. Cool thoroughly. Store in tightly covered containers.

Available in ethnic food sections of large supermarkets.

Note: Crackers may also be frozen up to 6 months. Re-crisp in a moderate oven (350°) for 8 to 10 minutes.

TEEN GRADUATION

Graduation from high school is a milestone in one's life and an occasion to celebrate proudly. A young host or hostess wishing to share the excitement with fellow classmates and family can easily prepare our menu.

DIPLOMA PARTY
Zippy Franks*
Chile Olive Dip* with Corn Chips
Spicy Nut Mix*
Yogurt Fruit Dip* with Strawberries
The Pack-Mouth Special*
UFO Sandwiches*
Barbecued Chicken Drumettes*
Pickles and Olives
Peanut Butter and Chocolate Granola Bars*
Ice Cream Sundae Bar
Vanilla or Chocolate Ice Cream
Chocolate Cherry Ice Cream Sauce*
Honeyed Orange-Nut Sauce*
Raisins, Nuts, Sunflower Seeds, Granola
Soft Drinks or Fruit Drinks
*Recipe given

ZIPPY FRANKS

Makes 8 servings.

- **1 jar (10 ounces) red currant jelly**
- **½ cup prepared mustard**
- **1 tablespoon prepared horseradish**
- **1 package (1 pound) frankfurters, cut into 1-inch pieces**

Melt jelly in a medium-size saucepan over low heat. Stir in mustard, horseradish and frankfurters. Heat and serve with wooden picks.

CHILE OLIVE DIP

Makes 1¾ cups.

- **¼ cup mayonnaise**
- **1 can (4 ounces) diced mild green chilies, drained**
- **½ cup pimiento-stuffed olives**
- **1 container (8 ounces) dairy sour cream**
- **½ teaspoon salt**
- **½ teaspoon chili powder**

1. Put mayonnaise, chilies and olives in the container of an electric blender; cover and whirl on medium speed until smooth.
2. Spoon sour cream into a small bowl and stir in mayonnaise mixture, salt and chili powder.
3. Cover and refrigerate 1 hour or longer until serving time.

SPICY NUT MIX

Bake at 300° for 15 minutes.
Makes about 4½ cups.

- **1 package (3¾ ounces) whole unblanched almonds**
- **2 cups square rice cereal**
- **1 cup sunflower seeds**
- **1½ tablespoons Worcestershire sauce**
- **1 tablespoon vegetable oil**
- **¼ teaspoon chili powder**
- **Pinch garlic powder**
- **Salt and pepper**

1. Put almonds, rice cereal and sunflower seeds into a large bowl. Add Worcestershire sauce, oil, chili powder and garlic powder; toss to mix well. Spread mixture on a large cookie sheet or jelly-roll pan.
2. Bake in a slow oven (300°) for 15 minutes. Remove from oven; cool completely. Season with salt and pepper.
3. Store in an airtight container in a dark cool place.

YOGURT FRUIT DIP

This fruit dip platter can be served as an appetizer or as a light, refreshing dessert.

Makes 2 cups.

- **1 container (8 ounces) plain yogurt**
- **1 container (8 ounces) dairy sour cream**
- **2 tablespoons honey**
- **¾ teaspoon ground ginger**
- **½ teaspoon lemon juice**

Blend all ingredients in a small bowl until smooth. Cover and refrigerate 1 hour or longer to chill thoroughly and blend flavors.
Dipper Tips: Good with whole strawberries, pineapple chunks, tiny bunches of seedless grapes, melon wedges, banana, apple and pear slices. To prevent discoloring, dip banana, apple and pear slices in lemon juice before arranging on platter.

THE PACK-MOUTH SPECIAL

Hero, hoagie, submarine, whatever you call it, this sandwich (of salami, mortadella, Provolone, lettuce, peppers and caper dressing) makes a delicious, hearty mouthful.

Makes 6 servings.

- **2 tablespoons tarragon vinegar**
- **2 tablespoons olive or vegetable oil**
- **1 tablespoon drained capers (optional)**
- **¼ teaspoon Italian herb seasoning mix, crumbled**
- **1 large loaf sesame-seeded French or Italian bread (about 15 inches long)**

- **1 cup shredded iceberg lettuce**
- **1 package (12 ounces) sliced cotto salami**
- **½ pound sliced mortadella**
- **1 package (8 ounces) sliced Provolone cheese, cut in half**
- **1 small sweet red pepper, halved, seeded and cut into thin strips**
- **1 small green pepper, halved, seeded and cut into thin strips**

1. Combine vinegar, oil, capers, if using, and Italian herb seasoning in a 1-cup measure; stir until blended.
2. Cut slice from top of loaf; reserve. Scoop out center of bottom half. (Reserve bread to make crumbs.)
3. Fill bottom of loaf with shredded lettuce. Stir dressing and drizzle half over lettuce. Fold salami and mortadella in quarters. Arrange salami, mortadella and cheese over lettuce. Top with pepper strips. Drizzle with remaining dressing. Cover with reserved top of loaf. Cut into serving-size portions.

UFO SANDWICHES

Slivers of corned beef, pastrami and Swiss cheese are tucked into crisp mini round rolls and served in twos.

Makes 4 servings.

- **3 tablespoons butter or margarine, softened**
- **1 tablespoon prepared horseradish-mustard**
- **8 small brown-and-serve sourdough rolls**
- **2 packages (3 ounces each) sliced corned beef**
- **2 packages (3 ounces each) sliced pastrami**
- **1 package (6 ounces) sliced Swiss cheese, cut into quarters**

1. Combine butter and horseradish-mustard in a small bowl. Cut rolls almost in half, but do not separate. Spread mustard-butter on cut rolls; close and press down tops. Place on large cookie sheet.
2. Remove corned beef and pastrami from original packaging. Tear off two large pieces of aluminum foil; close securely; place on cookie sheet with rolls.
3. Bake rolls following label directions, heating meat at same time and temperature.
4. To assemble: Place 2 strips of Swiss cheese on bottom halves of rolls; divide corned beef on 4 rolls, pastrami on remaining rolls. Press down tops of rolls. Serve two sandwiches, one corned beef and one pastrami per serving, with sour pickles, if you wish.

BARBECUED CHICKEN DRUMETTES

Makes about 12 servings.
Bake at 350° for 40 minutes.

- **3 pounds chicken wings**
- **½ teaspoon salt**
- **¼ teaspoon pepper**
- **¼ cup vegetable oil**
- **1 large onion, chopped (1 cup)**
- **2 cloves garlic, chopped**
- **1 cup catsup**
- **½ cup apricot preserves**
- **1 tablespoon Worcestershire sauce**
- **¼ teaspoon liquid hot pepper seasoning**

1. Remove tips of chicken wings. Cut each wing into 2 pieces; sprinkle with salt and pepper. Place pieces side by side in a shallow glass dish.
2. Heat oil in a large skillet; sauté onion and garlic until golden, about 5 minutes. Stir in remaining ingredients; simmer 5 minutes. Cool and pour mixture evenly over chicken wings; chill for several hours or overnight.
3. When ready to serve, place wings in a single layer in a foil-lined shallow baking pan. Bake in a moderate oven (350°) for 40 minutes or until wings are tender. Serve hot.

PEANUT BUTTER AND CHOCOLATE GRANOLA BARS

An easy no-bake snack bar.

Makes 40 bars.

- **1 cup light corn syrup**
- **1 cup chunk-style peanut butter**
- **1 teaspoon vanilla**
- **1 cup instant nonfat dry milk**
- **1 cup raisins**
- **1 box (16 ounces) granola with almonds**
- **1 package (6 ounces) semisweet chocolate pieces**

1. Line the bottom of a 13 × 9 × 2-inch baking pan with wax paper.
2. Bring corn syrup to boiling in a 3-quart saucepan; add peanut butter, stirring until melted; remove from heat. Stir in vanilla and dry milk. Add the raisins and all but 1 cup of the granola; mix thoroughly. Add chocolate, stirring quickly just to mix. Chocolate will melt so do not overmix. (Bars should be rippled with chocolate.)
3. Transfer granola mixture to prepared pan and press firmly into a flat layer. Sprinkle with reserved granola, pressing down firmly. Refrigerate 30 minutes.
4. Cut granola into 40 bars using a sharp knife; refrigerate bars 30 minutes longer.

Salad Bar Buffet: Stuffed Dutch Edam, page 117

CHOCOLATE CHERRY ICE CREAM SAUCE

Ladle a warm river of this hot fudge and cherry sauce over vanilla or chocolate ice cream.

Makes about 3 cups.

- **4 squares unsweetened chocolate**
- **2 tablespoons butter or margarine**
- **¾ cup boiling water**
- **2 cups sugar**
- **3 tablespoons light corn syrup**
- **2 teaspoons vanilla**
- **1 jar (10 ounces) maraschino cherries, well drained**

1. Coarsely chop chocolate; heat with butter and boiling water in a large heavy saucepan over low heat, stirring constantly until chocolate is melted. Add sugar and corn syrup.
2. Bring mixture slowly to boiling; lower heat; simmer gently 15 minutes. Watch carefully, but do not stir. Test on ice cream or an ice cube until it firms up as you like it. Add vanilla and well-drained cherries. Serve warm. Refrigerate any leftover sauce in screw-top jar.
3. *To reheat:* Remove cover from jar. Place jar in saucepan of water. Heat over low heat, stirring occasionally, until sauce is just softened enough to pour.

HONEYED ORANGE-NUT SAUCE

Makes about 6 cups.

- **1 cup light corn syrup**
- **1 tablespoon grated orange rind**
- **1 cup orange juice**
- **2 cups honey**
- **1 package (2½ ounces) whole shelled filberts (hazelnuts)**
- **1 can (6 ounces) pecan halves**
- **1 can (3½ ounces) whole blanched almonds**
- **½ pound walnut pieces**

Combine corn syrup, orange rind, orange juice and honey in large saucepan. Cook just until mixture comes to boiling. Remove from heat; add filberts, pecans, almonds and walnuts. Blend well. Chill.

A HOMECOMING PARTY

When a member of your family returns for a visit or has been away at school, welcome him back with a casual party set up as a salad bar buffet. It's relatively inexpensive and because everything can be prepared ahead and guests serve themselves, you won't miss out on any of the fun. Have the party for lunch or dinner and set it outside on the patio table if weather permits. It's really a great way to entertain. With the trend towards light eating, low-calorie foods and casual living, this is the perfect choice. Offer a selection of greens, garnishes and different dressings so that your guests can make a whole meal. Add breads or croutons as super filler-uppers. For dessert, set out filled cream puffs or fresh fruit. Since wine does not stand up to salads, serve light beer, sparkling mineral water or soft drinks.

SALAD BAR BUFFET
Mixed Salad Greens
Herb Vinaigrette Dressing*
Creamy Italian Dressing*
Low-Calorie Creamy Yogurt Dressing*
Cashew Dressing*
Dilled Potato Salad*
Ratatouille with Pita Bread*
Ham in Parsley Jelly*
Stuffed Dutch Edam*
Individual Parmesan-Onion Rolls*
Banana-Honey-Bran Bread*
Cheese Sticks
Profiteroles au Chocolat
Fresh Fruit
Beer   Sparkling Water
Soft Drinks
*Recipe given

FOR A BASIC SALAD BAR

Salad Greens: *Allow 1 to 1½ cups per serving.* Choose two or more of the following: Arugula (rocket); Bibb (limestone); Boston (butterhead); cabbage (Chinese, green and red); chicory (curly endive); dandelions; endive; escarole; iceberg; leaf (garden) lettuce; romaine (cos); spinach and watercress.

Dressings: Offer three or more bottled, packaged or homemade dressings. *Allow ¼ cup per serving.* Suggestions: Blue cheese, buttermilk-cucumber, Caesar, creamy cottage cheese or Roquefort, dilled sour cream, French, garlic-anchovy, green goddess, Italian, low-calorie herbed tomato, minted yogurt, old-fashioned cooked, Thousand Island and vinaigrette.

Raw and Cooked Vegetables: *Allow 1 cup per serving.* Suggestions: artichoke hearts (cooked or marinated); asparagus spears (cooked); avocado (cubed or sliced, raw); bamboo shoots (canned); bean sprouts (canned or fresh); beets (diced or sliced, cooked or pickled); broccoli and cauliflower flowerets (raw); carrots (shredded, sliced or slivered, raw); cucumbers (peeled or unpeeled, sliced or cubed, raw); green beans (cut up, cooked or dilled); green peas (cooked); mushrooms (whole caps or sliced, raw); onions (chopped or sliced, raw); peppers (red or green, cubed or sliced, raw); potatoes (sliced or cubed, cooked); tomatoes (sliced, raw); turnips (sliced, raw) water chestnuts; zucchini (sliced, raw or cooked).

Protein Foods: *Allow 1 cup per serving.* *Cheese:* Bel Paese, blue, brick, Cheddar, Colby, cream, Edam, feta, Gorgonzola, Gouda, Monterey Jack, Muenster, Port du Salut, Roquefort, Swiss. *Meats:* Beef, lamb, pork, veal, salami, pepperoni, liverwurst, deviled ham, bologna, other cold cuts (cubes, strips or sliced). *Seafood:* Crabmeat, fish, lobster, shrimp, salmon, smoked oysters, sardines, herring. *Legumes:* Beans (canned or dried, cooked), chick-peas, green limas, lentils. *Miscellaneous:* Bean curd, hard-cooked eggs (slices or wedges).

Fruits: *Allow 1 cup per serving* (fresh, cooked, canned). Apples (diced, sliced, unpeeled); cantaloupe; honeydew; Persian melon; cranshaw melon; watermelon (slices, wedges, balls); grapefruit and orange (segments); grapes; bananas (sliced or diced); peaches or nectarines (sliced); dates; prunes; apricots; blueberries; kiwi.

Toppings: *Allow 1 to 2 tablespoons per serving.* Croutons, chives, pumpkin seeds, bacon pieces, rolled or flat anchovies, walnuts, pecans, almonds, cashews, pistachios, pine nuts, macadamia nuts, peanuts, pumpkin and sunflower seeds, raisins, chutney, capers.

HERB VINAIGRETTE DRESSING

Makes 1¼ cups.

- **¾ cup vegetable oil**
- **½ cup tarragon-flavored vinegar**
- **¾ teaspoon salt**
- **¼ teaspoon seasoned pepper**
- **¼ teaspoon leaf basil, crumbled**

Shake all ingredients in a screw-top jar. Refrigerate to mellow flavors. Shake again just before pouring over salad.

CREAMY ITALIAN DRESSING

Makes about 1½ cups.

- **1 egg**
- **1 tablespoon Dijon mustard**
- **½ small onion**
- **½ teaspoon salt**
- **¼ teaspoon pepper**
- **1 clove garlic**
- **⅛ teaspoon sugar**
- **2 tablespoons lemon juice**
- **¼ cup red wine vinegar**
- **1 cup olive or vegetable oil**

1. Combine egg, mustard, onion, salt, pepper, garlic, sugar, lemon juice and vinegar in the container of an electric blender; cover. Whirl until smooth.
2. Add oil slowly through center of blender cover while blender is running. Dressing will be quite thick. Refrigerate at least 1 hour to blend flavors.

LOW-CALORIE CREAMY YOGURT DRESSING

Makes 1 cup.

- **1 container (8 ounces) plain yogurt**
- **2 tablespoons lemon juice**
- **¼ cup minced green onions**
- **2 tablespoons grated Parmesan cheese**
- **2 tablespoons finely snipped fresh dill**
- **OR: 2 teaspoons dillweed**
- **¾ teaspoon salt**
- **¼ teaspoon white pepper**

Combine yogurt, lemon juice, onions, Parmesan, dill, salt and pepper in a medium-size bowl; mix well until creamy. Cover; refrigerate 2 hours or longer to blend flavors. Stir before serving.

CASHEW DRESSING

Delicious over salad greens, vegetables or tomatoes.

Makes about 2 cups.

- **1 cup raw cashews or dry-roasted cashews**
- **½ cup vegetable oil**
- **½ cup water**
- **2 tablespoons lemon juice**
- **1 tablespoon tamari or soy sauce**
- **1½ teaspoons fresh dill, chopped**
- **1½ teaspoons honey**

Place all ingredients in the container of an electric blender. Cover; whirl until smooth. Turn mixture into screw-top jar. Refrigerate several hours for flavors to blend.

DILLED POTATO SALAD

New potatoes are served whole with this special sour cream and dill dressing.

Makes 4 to 6 servings.

- **12 tiny new potatoes**
- **2 tablespoons vegetable oil**
- **2 tablespoons lemon juice**
- **2 teaspoons salt**
- **¼ teaspoon pepper**
- **2 tablespoons chopped fresh dill**
- **OR: 2 teaspoons dillweed**
- **1 large cucumber, pared, quartered, seeded and chopped**
- **¾ cup dairy sour cream**
- **Iceberg lettuce**

1. Cook potatoes just until tender, about 15 minutes, in boiling salted water in a large saucepan; drain. Peel potatoes and

return to saucepan; toss over very low heat 5 minutes to dry. Place in a large bowl.
2. Combine oil, lemon juice, salt, pepper and dill in a jar with a screwtop; cover and shake well; pour over potatoes and toss to coat. Cover bowl with plastic wrap and chill at least 3 hours.
3. Just before serving, toss potatoes with cucumber and sour cream. Line a salad bowl with iceberg lettuce; fill with salad; garnish with a sprig of fresh dill.

RATATOUILLE WITH PITA BREAD

Makes about 6 cups filling.

- **2 tablespoons olive oil**
- **1 large onion, chopped (1 cup)**
- **2 cloves garlic, chopped**
- **1 green pepper, halved, seeded and chopped**
- **2 ripe tomatoes, chopped**
- **2 zucchini, trimmed and chopped**
- **1 medium-size unpeeled eggplant, chopped**
- **½ teaspoon leaf basil, crumbled**
- **1½ teaspoons leaf oregano, crumbled**
- **1 cup tomato juice**
- **¼ cup bottled Italian salad dressing**
- **2 teaspoons salt**
- **½ teaspoon pepper**
- **12 small or medium pita bread, quartered**
- **Chopped fresh parsley**

1. Heat oil in a large saucepan or Dutch oven; sauté onion, garlic and green pepper until soft, about 5 minutes. Stir in tomatoes, zucchini, eggplant, basil, oregano, tomato juice, salad dressing, salt and pepper. Simmer, stirring occasionally, until mixture is thick and vegetables are soft, about 20 minutes. Cool; chill.
2. When ready to serve, fill a large bowl with ratatouille. Surround bowl with pita. Sprinkle ratatouille with parsley and use a spoon to fill pita as they are served.

HAM IN PARSLEY JELLY

This combination of ham, parsley and aspic or jelly is a classic dish made easy.

Makes 8 servings.

- **2 envelopes unflavored gelatin**
- **2 cans condensed chicken broth**
- **1 cup water**
- **½ cup Madeira wine**
- **2 tablespoons lemon juice**
- **1 tablespoon vinegar**
- **1 teaspoon leaf tarragon, crumbled**

1 pound boiled ham, cut ¼-inch thick and diced (3 cups)
1 cup chopped fresh parsley

1. Sprinkle gelatin over chicken broth and water in a medium-size saucepan; heat, stirring constantly, until gelatin dissolves. Pour into a large bowl; stir in Madeira, lemon juice, vinegar and tarragon.
2. Set bowl in larger pan of ice and water to speed setting. Chill, stirring frequently, just until mixture is as thick as unbeaten egg whites.
3. Fold in ham and parsley; spoon into an 8-cup mold. Chill several hours or until firm.
4. To unmold: Run a sharp thin-bladed knife around top of mold, then dip mold very quickly in and out of a pan of warm water. Cover mold with serving plate; invert; carefully lift off mold. Garnish with watercress and tomato roses, if you wish.

STUFFED DUTCH EDAM
Makes 3 cups.

1 Dutch Edam cheese, about 2 pounds
2 tablespoons prepared horseradish
1 container (8 ounces) dairy sour cream
½ cup undrained pickle relish
6 bacon slices, crisp-fried and crumbled
Carrots, cut in thin diagonal pieces
Green pepper, seeded and cut in 1-inch strips
Celery, cut in diagonal pieces
Zucchini, thinly sliced
Mushrooms, cut in thick slices

1. Cut ½ inch off top of Edam; scoop out center with a sharp knife and then a spoon, leaving a shell about ½-inch thick; wrap and chill. Shred removed cheese and place in a bowl; stir in horseradish, sour cream, pickle relish and bacon; beat until well blended; chill.
2. Wrap and chill vegetables.
3. When ready to serve, place cheese shell on a serving platter and fill with cheese dip. (For best flavor, allow cheese dip to warm to room temperature before filling shell.) Arrange vegetables around cheese shell. Refill shell with remaining dip as needed.

INDIVIDUAL PARMESAN-ONION ROLLS
Bake at 400° for 7 minutes.
Makes 12 rolls.

12 Italian or hero round hard rolls OR: 4 long hero rolls (7 to 8 inches each), halved and split lengthwise
½ cup (1 stick) butter or margarine, softened
1½ tablespoons instant minced onion
⅓ cup grated Parmesan cheese
2 tablespoons chopped parsley (optional)

1. Split rolls horizontally.
2. Combine butter and onion; mix well. Spread cut surfaces of rolls with butter-onion mixture. Arrange rolls on a cookie sheet.
3. Bake in a hot oven (400°) for 5 minutes. Remove from oven and sprinkle with some Parmesan and chopped parsley, if used. Return to oven 2 minutes.

BANANA-HONEY-BRAN BREAD
A nice moist bread that keeps well.
Bake at 350° for 1 hour.
Makes 1 loaf.

1½ cups *sifted* all-purpose flour
2 teaspoons baking powder
½ teaspoon baking soda
½ teaspoon salt
1 cup whole bran cereal
¼ cup chopped walnuts
1 egg
½ cup honey
¼ cup vegetable oil
¼ cup milk
1½ cups mashed ripe bananas

1. Preheat oven to 350°. Sift flour, baking powder, baking soda and salt into a large bowl. Stir in cereal and walnuts.
2. Beat egg slightly in a small bowl, then beat in honey, oil, milk and bananas.
3. Add banana mixture all at once to dry ingredients and stir just until flour is dampened. Spoon batter into a greased 9 × 5 × 3-inch loaf pan.
4. Bake in a preheated moderate oven (350°) for 1 hour or until a wooden pick inserted in center comes out clean. Cool in pan on wire rack 10 minutes. Remove from pan; cool completely. Wrap in foil or plastic; when cool, store overnight.

PROFITEROLES AU CHOCOLAT
Bake at 400° for 30 minutes.
Makes 36 puffs (3 per serving).

1 cup water
½ cup (1 stick) butter or margarine
1 teaspoon sugar
¼ teaspoon salt
1 cup *sifted* all-purpose flour
4 eggs

Whipped Cocoa Cream (*recipe follows*)
Chocolate Sauce (*recipe follows*)

1. Heat water, butter, sugar and salt to a full rolling boil in a medium-size saucepan.
2. Add flour all at once. Stir vigorously with a wooden spoon until mixture forms a thick, smooth ball that follows spoon around and leaves side of pan clean (about 1 minute). Remove from heat; cool slightly.
3. Preheat oven to 400°. Add eggs, 1 at a time, beating well after each addition until paste is shiny and smooth. Spoon in small mounds, using a slightly rounded teaspoon for each, onto ungreased cookie sheets, 1 inch apart.
4. Bake in a preheated hot oven (400°) for 30 minutes or until puffed and golden. Cool completely on wire rack.
5. Make Whipped Cocoa Cream.
6. To fill puffs: Make a small hole in side or bottom of each puff. Fit pastry bag with plain tip. Spoon filling into bag. Press filling into cream puffs. Or, cut a slice from top of each puff, then spoon filling in; replace tops.
7. Pile puffs into shallow serving bowl; drizzle warm Chocolate Sauce over.

Note: If you wish, profiteroles can be filled with vanilla ice cream. Keep frozen until ready to serve. Serve with warm Chocolate Sauce drizzled over.

WHIPPED COCOA CREAM
Makes 4 cups.

2 cups heavy cream
⅔ cup 10X (confectioners') sugar
½ cup unsweetened cocoa powder
1 teaspoon vanilla

Combine ingredients in a deep, medium-size bowl; beat with rotary hand beater or electric mixer just until stiff.

CHOCOLATE SAUCE
Makes 1¼ cups.

½ cup milk
¼ cup sugar
4 squares semisweet chocolate
1 square unsweetened chocolate
1 tablespoon butter or margarine
1 teaspoon vanilla

Combine milk and sugar in top of double boiler; cook over boiling water until sugar dissolves. Remove from heat but leave top of boiler over water in bottom. Add chocolate and butter. Stir until melted; stir in vanilla. Serve warm. Sauce can be made ahead of time; then reheated over hot water.

HOT TIPS FOR A COLD SALAD BAR

1. If you don't use the crispest, freshest greens, a salad bar can be a disaster. So be fussy and pick those at their peak. Look for a good green color, few if any blemishes and as little dirt as possible.

2. Salad greens gain extra crispness if refrigerated overnight. Rinse leafy greens (Bibb, romaine, Boston, chicory, arugula and spinach) as soon as you've brought them home. Trim any wilted or bruised leaves. Pat dry on paper toweling or whirl in a salad spinner or wire basket. Store in plastic bags. Don't wash iceberg—trim and store in hydrator.

3. Tear salad greens into bite-size pieces to fill your largest salad bowl. You can do this way ahead of time; just cover with plastic wrap or foil and keep refrigerated.

4. To save space yet offer the largest possible selection, arrange several ingredients in a single container, selecting them for colors and shapes that complement each other.

HAPPY ANNIVERSARY

An anniversary, a wedding, a new job or any happy occasion, calls for a special dinner. Congratulate the guest or guests of honor with an intimate gathering of family or close friends. If you plan on a large group, just prepare the dishes in quantity and serve them buffet style.

> **ANNIVERSARY DINNER**
> **Salmon Mousse***
> **Shrimp-Stuffed Eggs***
> **Chicken Braised in**
> **Champagne***
> **Pan-Roasted Potatoes**
> **Acorn Squash with Broccoli**
> **Puree***
> **Fresh Fruit Salad***
> **with Orange-Yogurt Dressing***
> **Appliqué Anniversary Cake***
> **Sparkling Wine or Cider**
> *Recipe given

SALMON MOUSSE

Makes 8 servings.

- 1 envelope unflavored gelatin
- ¼ cup cold water
- ½ cup boiling water
- ½ cup mayonnaise
- 1 tablespoon lemon juice
- 1 tablespoon grated onion
- ½ teaspoon liquid hot pepper seasoning
- 1 teaspoon salt
- 1 can (15½ ounces) red salmon
- ½ cup heavy cream, whipped

1. Sprinkle gelatin over cold water to soft-en in a large bowl, about 5 minutes. Add boiling water; stir until dissolved Let cool 5 minutes.

2. Add mayonnaise, lemon juice, onion, hot pepper seasoning and salt. Mix until well blended. Chill until the consistency of unbeaten egg white.

3. Drain salmon and puree in blender. Fold into chilled gelatin mixture.

4. Gently fold whipped cream into salmon mixture. Turn into a 4-cup mold.

5. Refrigerate until firm, about 4 hours or overnight.

6. Unmold and garnish with sprigs of fresh dill, if you wish.

SHRIMP-STUFFED EGGS

Makes 8 servings.

- 8 hard-cooked eggs
- ½ cup mayonnaise
- 1 tablespoon chopped fresh dill
- ¼ teaspoon salt
- 1 jar (about 4 ounces) shrimp, drained

1. Halve eggs lengthwise; scoop out yolks into a bowl. Mash yolks thoroughly with a fork or pastry blender.

2. Beat in mayonnaise, dill and salt.

3. Reserve 16 whole shrimp. Chop remaining shrimp finely. Fold into yolk mixture.

4. Refill whites; garnish with reserved shrimp and fresh dill sprigs. Refrigerate.

CHICKEN BRAISED IN CHAMPAGNE

Bake at 400° for 50 minutes, then at 325° for 1 hour.
Makes 6 servings.

- 1 roasting chicken (about 5 pounds)
- 1½ teaspoons salt
- ¼ teaspoon pepper
- 1 teaspoon lemon juice
- ½ teaspoon leaf tarragon, crumbled
- 2 tablespoons chopped fresh parsley
- ¼ cup (½ stick) butter or margarine, softened
- 4 small yellow onions, quartered
- 2 pounds small new potatoes
- 1¾ cups champagne
- 2 tablespoons flour

1. Wash chicken; pat dry with paper toweling. Sprinkle inside with 1 teaspoon of the salt and the pepper. Beat remaining salt, lemon juice, tarragon and parsley into butter in a small bowl.

2. Loosen breast skin from chicken; place about 1 tablespoon of butter mixture under skin on each side; tie legs of chicken together. Rub remaining butter mix-ture over chicken. Place in small roasting pan.

3. Roast, uncovered, in a hot oven (400°) for 50 minutes. Add onions and potatoes to roasting pan. Pour 1½ cups of the champagne over. Cover pan tightly with foil. Lower oven temperature to 325°. Braise, covered, basting several times, 1 hour longer or until chicken and vegetables are tender.

4. Remove chicken to a heated platter. Make a smooth paste with flour and remaining ¼ cup champagne. Pour into pan liquid. Cook over medium heat, stirring constantly, until thickened and bubbly. Cook 2 minutes; taste and add more salt, if needed. Serve with chicken.

ACORN SQUASH WITH BROCCOLI PUREE

Bake at 375° for 55 minutes.
Makes 8 servings.

- 2 large acorn squash (about 4 pounds)
- ¼ cup (½ stick) butter or margarine
- ½ teaspoon salt
- ¼ teaspoon pepper
- 1 bunch (1 pound) broccoli
- ½ teaspoon salt
- ⅛ teaspoon pepper
- ¼ cup (½ stick) butter or margarine

1. Cut each squash into quarters; scoop out seeds. Place each piece, hollow-side up, on a square of aluminum foil large enough to enclose it. Dot each piece with butter. Sprinkle each with salt and pepper. Fold foil tightly around squash. Squash may be refrigerated in foil if made ahead. Place on cookie sheet.

2. Bake in a moderate oven (375°) for 45 minutes or until squash is tender.

3. Trim broccoli of stem ends and leaves. Wash and separate into stalks and pieces of equal size. Cover with boiling water; add salt and pepper. Simmer, covered, for 15 minutes or until tender. Drain thoroughly; return to pan. Add butter and shake over very low heat just until butter melts. Turn into container of electric blender. Puree. Puree may be refrigerated at this point, if making ahead. Pipe puree through a pastry bag onto baked squash. Return to oven for 10 minutes or until thoroughly heated.

Anniversary Dinner: Chicken Braised in Champagne, page 118; Fresh Fruit Salad, page 120; Salmon Mousse, page 118

FRESH FRUIT SALAD WITH ORANGE YOGURT DRESSING

Makes 8 servings.

Romaine lettuce leaves
2 navel oranges, pared and sectioned
2 grapefruit, pared and sectioned
2 large avocados
Lemon juice
2 large fresh pears
⅓ cup chopped macadamia nuts or walnuts
Watercress
Orange-Yogurt Dressing (recipe follows)

1. Line serving platter with crisp, chilled romaine leaves. Arrange orange and grapefruit sections alternately in spoke fashion.
2. Peel and pit avocados; slice; sprinkle with lemon juice. Core pears, from bottom, keeping pears whole. Cut into crosswise slices. Brush each with lemon juice. Arrange on platter.
3. Sprinkle chopped nuts over arranged fruits. Garnish with watercress. Serve with Orange-Yogurt Dressing.

ORANGE YOGURT DRESSING

Makes about 2 cups.

½ cup sugar
1 tablespoon cornstarch
¼ teaspoon salt
1 teaspoon grated orange rind
1 cup orange juice
2 eggs, beaten
1 container (8 ounces) plain yogurt

1. Combine sugar, cornstarch and salt in small saucepan. Stir in orange rind and juice. Cook over medium heat, stirring constantly, until thickened and clear.
2. Stir about ¼ cup of juice mixture slowly into beaten eggs in a small bowl. Return to saucepan. Cook about 1 minute longer. Refrigerate until thoroughly cold. Fold in yogurt. Refrigerate.

APPLIQUÉ ANNIVERSARY CAKE

You can't make a mistake when decorating this cake. All the decorations are easy to shape on paper, then peel off and place on the cake just where you want them.

Makes 18 servings.

2 packages yellow cake mix
Royal Frosting (recipe follows)
Red food coloring
Silver dragees
2 containers (16.5 ounces each) vanilla ready-to-spread frosting

1. Prepare, bake and cool one cake mix for a 13 × 9 × 2-inch cake. Prepare, bake and cool remaining cake mix for two 9 × 1½-inch layers. Reserve one layer for another dessert. Level tops of all cakes with a serrated knife.
2. Cut a 5-inch round and a 7-inch round from the 13 × 9 × 2-inch cake, using a saucer.
3. Write or trace HAPPY ANNIVERSARY on a sheet of wax paper, allowing a ½-inch space between letters. Tape paper to a cookie sheet. Tape a sheet of wax paper on top of taped sheet.
4. Prepare Royal Frosting; tint light pink with food coloring. Cover bowl with a damp towel to keep frosting moist.
5. Fit a pastry bag with a small to medium-size open star tube. Trace letters with either a straight line or a series of connecting rosettes. Make sure all rosettes in the letter touch each other. If you make a mistake, it's easy to scrape off the frosting and start again. Pipe out about 50 teardrops* onto paper. Pipe out 40 spirals,* placing a silver dragee in center of each. Pipe out as many spirals, just a bit larger, to match the years you are celebrating. These will be candle holders; put a birthday candle in center of each. Allow decorations to dry for at least 2 hours.
6. Place the 9-inch layer on serving plate. Frost side and top with part of the vanilla frosting. Center 7-inch layer; frost. Top with 5-inch layer; frost.
7. Gently loosen decorations with a thin metal spatula or knife. Arrange letters for HAPPY on middle tier. Arrange ANNIVERSARY on lower tier. Place remaining decorations, except candle holders, in bow tie patterns, one spiral between two teardrops, around the vertical sides of the tiers. Space candles and holders on top.

*See ''Cakes for Special Occasions.''

ROYAL FROSTING

Makes about 2 cups.

2 egg whites
¼ teaspoon cream of tartar
2½ to 3 cups 10X (confectioners') sugar

Beat egg whites and cream of tartar in small bowl until foamy. Gradually beat in sugar until frosting stands in firm peaks and is stiff enough to hold its shape when cut through with a knife. (Keep bowl covered with damp paper toweling while working to keep frosting from drying out.)

CHILDREN'S BIRTHDAY

Delight the young set with this easy party menu. Your early school-age child can help with some of the party preparations. For instance, he or she can easily help prepare the tiny sandwiches. After school, between 3:30 and 5:30 p.m., is probably the best party time. Postponing the party until the weekend is not quite the same to the guest of honor. Be sure to have plenty of games, prizes, balloons and party hats!

CHILDREN'S BIRTHDAY PARTY
Popcorn
Double-Good Tiny Sandwiches*
Pineapple Punch*
Calico Cat Cake*
Strawberry Ice Cream
*Recipe given

DOUBLE-GOOD TINY SANDWICHES

Two delicious easy-mix fillings.

Makes 2 dozen small sandwiches.

18 slices white bread (from a 1½-pound loaf)
¼ cup (½ stick) butter or margarine, softened
Ham Filling (recipe follows)
Cheese Filling (recipe follows)

1. Spread bread slices with softened butter; arrange in 3 rows of 6 slices each. Spread first row with Ham Filling. Cover with slices in second row, butter-side down. Spread unbuttered sides with Cheese Filling. Top with remaining slices, butter-side down, to make 6 sandwiches. Wrap in wax paper, foil or plastic wrap; chill.
2. Unwrap sandwiches; trim crusts if you wish; cut each sandwich into quarters.

Ham Filling: Combine 1 can deviled ham (4½ ounces) with 2 teaspoons mayonnaise or salad dressing and ½ teaspoon prepared mustard in a bowl. Makes about ⅓ cup.

Cheese Filling: Cream 1 package (3 ounces) softened cream cheese with 1 tablespoon grated Parmesan cheese, 1 teaspoon lemon juice and ⅛ teaspoon Worcestershire sauce to spreading consistency in small bowl. Makes about ⅓ cup.

PINEAPPLE PUNCH

Makes 6 servings.

4 cups unsweetened pineapple juice
2 tablespoons lemon juice
2 tablespoons lime juice
2 bottles (12 ounces each) club soda

Combine pineapple juice, lemon and lime juices in large pitcher. Stir to mix. Chill. Just before serving, add club soda. Pour over ice in 3 tall glasses. Garnish with lemon or lime slice and pineapple chunks, if you wish.

CALICO CAT CAKE

Makes 12 servings.

- **1 package yellow cake mix**
- **2 containers (16.5 ounces each) vanilla ready-to-spread frosting**
- **2 tablespoons unsweetened cocoa powder**
- **1 package small chocolate-covered mints Red and yellow food colorings**

1. Prepare, bake and cool cake mix following label directions for two 9 × 1½-inch layers. Level cooled cake layers with a serrated knife.

2. Place a 5½-inch bowl or saucer in the center of one layer. Cut out the circle to make the cat's head (B). Cut out ⅓ of the outer ring to form a curved cat's tail (C). Cut four 1½-inch triangles from the remaining ring to form ears (D) and the bow tie (E).

3. Assemble cat on a tray, placing small circle (B) above the 9-inch layer (A). Position the ears (D), then the tail (C). The bow tie will be frosted and placed on top of cake where the two circles meet. Extra piece of cake may be used as treat for the children.

4. Combine ½ cup of the vanilla frosting with cocoa in a small bowl. Stir in a little water, if needed, to thin.

5. Spread a small amount of vanilla frosting from the neck halfway down the large layer or body area to form a bib. Spread wide horizontal lines of white frosting across the body, tail and head with a small metal spatula, leaving space to spread alternating orange lines.

6. Tint remaining container of frosting a light orange with a few drops of red and yellow food coloring. Spread orange stripes in the spaces left between the white lines. Gently swirl stripes to blend and soften lines. Frost side of cake with the remaining orange frosting.

7. Frost bow tie with chocolate frosting; put in place. Put two chocolate mints in place for eyes. Pipe whiskers and a mouth with remaining chocolate frosting.

8. Fit a pastry bag with a small plain tube; fill with remaining vanilla frosting. Pipe a pair of glasses around eyes, and decorate bow tie.

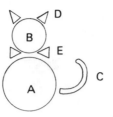

CAKES FOR SPECIAL OCCASIONS

A decorated cake always has a way of conveying a message for a special occasion. You don't have to be a master baker to create these cakes. Our techniques and shortcuts give you perfect results. Although a pastry bag or cake decorator with different tips or tubes is all that you will need in the way of special equipment, some of these cakes can be decorated without one.

HOW TO DECORATE A CAKE

● **Pastry Bag:** Fit required tip into pastry bag. Fill bag with frosting, pressing the frosting all the way to the end of the tip. Twist or fold the open end of the pastry bag to keep a slight amount of pressure on the frosting. Hold the bag at the twist or fold, between the thumb and forefinger of the right hand (or left hand, if left-handed). Guide the bag with the opposite hand.

Cake Decorator: Fit required tip on the cake decorating cylinder; fill tip with frosting. Gently press plunger to remove any air bubbles. Press plunger with an even steady pressure, guiding the tip with the opposite hand.

Wax-Paper Cone: Measure off a perfect 12-inch square of wax paper; fold diagonally; cut on diagonal fold. (You can make 2 cones from one square.) Using center of diagonal line as center point of cone, bring corners up and wrap around, closing tip of cone tightly; fasten cone with tape. Cut off just enough of the point of the cone to hold decorating tip snugly. Or, you can use the cone by itself for the simple plain designs.

DESIGNS

Wavy: Hold pastry bag with tip at a 45° angle to and almost touching cake. Squeeze with an even pressure, working from far edge to near edge in a push (up and away) and pull (down and toward) motion. At the completion of the border, release pressure; lift tip away.

Rosette: Hold the pastry bag with the tip at a 90° angle to and almost touching the cake. Squeeze with an even pressure forming the

size rosettes you wish. Release pressure; lift tip away.

Zigzag: Hold pastry bag with the tip at a 45° angle to and almost touching the cake. Squeeze with an even pressure back and forth (left to right) in a tight "S" pattern flat on the cake. At the completion of the border, release pressure; lift tip away.

Teardrop: Hold pastry bag with the tip at a 45° angle to and slightly above cake. Squeeze with an even pressure until frosting fans out. Ease up slightly on pressure and pull toward you, tapering off flow of frosting. Release pressure; lift tip away.

Ball: Hold pastry bag with the tip at a 90° angle to and almost touching cake. Squeeze with an even pressure to form the size ball you wish. Release pressure; lift tip away.

Spiral: Hold pastry bag with the tip at a 90° angle to and slightly above cake. Squeeze with even pressure in a circular motion and, at the same time, moving upward. Ease pressure as circle is completed Release pressure; lift tip away.

FATHER'S DAY WORD GAME CAKE

Spell out a greeting to Dad with chocolate mint letters.

Makes 16 servings.

- **1 package chocolate or yellow cake mix**
- **1 container (16.5 ounces) chocolate ready-to-spread frosting**
- **1 container (16.5 ounces) vanilla ready-to-spread frosting**
- **1 package (8 ounces) round chocolate-covered mints Yellow food coloring**

1. Prepare, bake and cool cake mix following label directions for a 13 × 9 × 2-inch cake. Level top of cake with a serrated knife. Frost cooled cake with all but ½ cup of the chocolate frosting.

2. Fit a pastry bag with a small plain tip; fill with ½ the container of vanilla frosting. Pipe lines on the cake dividing evenly into squares; 7 squares across the long side, 5 squares across the short side. Pipe HAPPY FATHER'S DAY on the chocolate mints, one letter to each mint.

3. Tint remaining vanilla frosting yellow with food coloring. Carefully spread yellow frosting randomly to simulate a word game board.

4. Place mint "tiles" on cake "board."

5. Fit a pastry bag with a small star tip; pipe a wavy border around top and bottom edges of cake with remaining chocolate frosting.

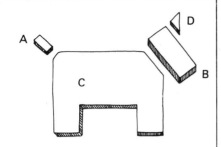

GINGHAM DOG CAKE

Make a wonderful patchwork of frosting patterns to adorn this perky little dog.

Makes 12 servings.

1 package yellow cake mix
2 containers (16.5 ounces each)
** vanilla ready-to-spread frosting**
1 package small
** chocolate-covered mints**

1. Prepare, bake and cool cake mix following label directions for 13 × 9 × 2-inch cake. Level with a serrated knife.
2. Measure off and cut a strip 3-inches wide from one of the short ends of the cake. Measure and cut a piece 3 × 1½-inches from this strip for a tail (D). Cut another piece from the strip, 5 × 3-inches for the head (E). Cut a small triangle off upper right corner of large rectangle to accommodate tail.
3. Mark off a 5 × 3-inch rectangle (B), evenly centered, along one long side of large rectangle body; cut out. Measure 1½ inches from upper left corner of body rectangle down each of the sides of rectangle; cut off the triangle (A) for the dog's ear; reserve.
4. Assemble pieces on a tray. Place head rectangle along upper left area of body (C) rectangle. Place ear triangle in place. Place tail in upper right area. Extra piece (B) of cake may be used as a treat for the children.

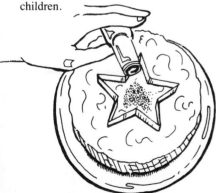

Cakes for Special Occasions: Father's Day Word Game Cake, page 121; Gingham Dog Cake, page 123; Fourth of July Star Cake, page 123

FOURTH OF JULY STAR CAKE

Makes 12 servings.

1 package yellow cake mix
2 containers (16.5 ounces each)
** vanilla ready-to-spread**
** frosting**
Red decorating sugar
Blue food coloring

1. Prepare, bake and cool cake mix following label directions for two 9 × 1½-inch layers. Level cake layers with a serrated knife. Assemble and frost cake with 1 container of the frosting.
2. Place a large star-shaped cookie cutter in the center of the frosted cake. Sprinkle red sugar evenly inside cutter. Press sugar lightly into frosting with fingertip. Gently remove cookie cutter.
3. Fit a pastry bag with a very small star tip. Fill bag with half of the remaining container of frosting. Pipe a rosette border outlining the star. Transfer remaining frosting to another pastry bag fitted with a small star tip. Pipe a rosette border around bottom of cake.
4. Tint remaining vanilla frosting blue with food coloring. Fit pastry bag with washed and dried small star tip. Pipe a zigzag border around top of cake.

ENCHANTED COTTAGE

This tiny pink cottage is surrounded by a shredded coconut "lawn" and fantasy "shrubs."

Bake at 350° for 25 minutes.
Makes 10 servings.

2 packages pound cake mix
⅓ cup apple jelly, melted
3 packages creamy vanilla
** frosting mix**
Red, yellow and green food
** colorings**
Flaked coconut

1. Grease two 15½ × 10½ × 1-inch jelly-roll pans; line bottoms with wax paper. Grease wax paper. (OR: Bake one cake at a time, re-using pan.)
2. Preheat oven to 350°. Prepare cake mixes following label directions. Turn batter into pans.
3. Bake in a preheated moderate oven (350°) for 25 minutes or until centers spring back when lightly pressed with fingertip.
4. Cool cakes in pans a few minutes; turn out onto wire racks. Remove wax paper. Cool completely.
5. Cut each cake into six squares (A). Put four cake squares together with melted jelly for base of house (B). Place on a 10 × 10-inch foil-covered cardboard square.

6. Put three cake squares together with melted jelly for "eaves" or roof support (C). Trim to wedge shape. Reserve cake trimmings. Spread top of house with remaining jelly; press "eaves" into position.
7. Prepare one package of frosting mix following label directions. Spread assembled cake with a very thin coat of frosting to hold crumbs in place. Allow to dry slightly.
8. Tint remaining frosting a deep pink. Frost entire cake except roof area. Reserve remaining frosting for Step 10.
9. Prepare second package of frosting mix; tint bright green. Spread one side of each of two cake squares with frosting. Position on "eaves"; hold in place with wooden picks. If roof does not quite meet at top, insert a strip of cake to fill the space. Spread roof with thin coat of frosting. Allow to dry slightly. Frost roof generously with overlapping strokes for "shingled" look.
10. Prepare third package of frosting mix. Divide into thirds; tint ⅓ green; ⅓ yellow and leave remaining third white. Cut "chimney" from "eave" trimmings so it fits roof angle. Top with a small piece of cake for height (D). Frost thinly with white frosting, then reserved pink frosting. Position on roof with wooden picks.
11. Spread cardboard with white frosting; sprinkle with green-tinted coconut. Pipe "windows," "shutters" and "door" with green frosting, using a small round tip fitted on cake decorator. With yellow frosting and small notched tip, pipe the "doorknob" and "chimney" decoration.
12. Cut small triangle shapes from remaining cake. Frost with green frosting; pipe on yellow "flowers." Place around cake for "landscaping."

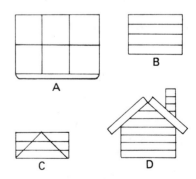

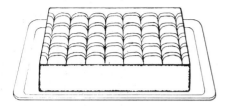

Feathertop

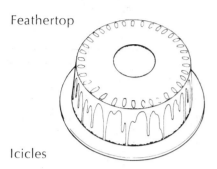

Icicles

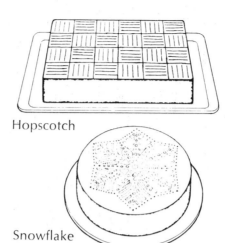

Hopscotch

Snowflake

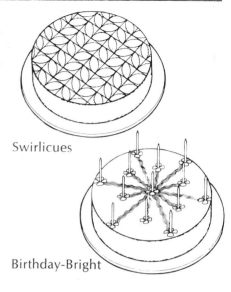

Swirlicues

Birthday-Bright

SIX WAYS TO DECORATE CAKES

Everyday kitchen tools—knife, fork, teaspoon, strainer, a lacy doily—are all you need. Creamy butter frostings, your own or from a mix, make the deep swirls and line designs shown. The other decorations are even easier.

Feathertop: Frost the cake all over with white frosting, then drizzle melted chocolate in thin lines, about 1 inch apart, across top. Draw knife through frosting and across chocolate to make this featherlike pattern.

Icicles: A simple 10X sugar-water frosting, just thin enough to pour from a spoon, is the topping here. Spoon the frosting over top of cake, letting it drip down around edge and inside the tube. Ring top with nuts.

Hopscotch: Frost an oblong or a square cake smoothly and let set until almost firm. Mark off the top evenly into squares with a knife, then, with tines of fork, press lines in each square, alternating their direction.

Snowflake: A pretty lacy doily is your "decorator" here. Place the doily on unfrosted cake, then fill tea strainer with 10X (confectioners') sugar; tap out thickly and evenly over top. Lift doily off.

Swirlicues: Spread a thick frosting over top. (It doesn't have to be smooth.) With tip of knife, draw straight lines, about 1 inch apart, across top; turn cake a quarter and draw a second set of lines. With tip of a spatula, shape leaves, reversing direction of each row.

Birthday-Bright: Out of candle holders? Make your own with ready-to-press-out frosting from a pressurized can. Using the flower tip, pipe out frosting in lines radiating from the center, as shown, then finish off with tiny rosettes.

GOURMET GIFTS FROM YOUR KITCHEN

Holidays mean entertaining and a time to exchange gifts. If you're in need of a special hostess gift or a special gift for some other occasion, we've got some delicious ones here. Food gifts from your kitchen tell friends and relatives, "You're something special!" Our edible gourmet gifts include fruitcakes, fabulous cheese spreads, candies, cookies and even a scrumptious steamed pudding. To make them more special, place in pretty wrappings or containers.

DATE-APRICOT STEAMED PUDDING

Moist, tender and chock-full of tangy dried fruits.
Makes 6 servings.

1 package (6 ounces) dried apricots, chopped
½ cup pitted dates, chopped
2 cups *sifted* all-purpose flour
1½ teaspoons baking powder
½ teaspoon baking soda
½ teaspoon salt
¾ teaspoon ground cinnamon
¼ teaspoon ground nutmeg
½ cup vegetable shortening
1 cup firmly packed light brown sugar
2 eggs
⅓ cup orange juice
Orange Custard Sauce *(recipe follows)*

1. Grease an 8-cup tube pan or pudding mold; dust with sugar.
2. Simmer apricots in boiling water 5 minutes; drain. Combine apricots and dates in a small bowl.
3. Sift flour, baking powder, baking soda, salt, cinnamon and nutmeg onto wax paper.
4. Beat shortening, sugar and eggs in a large bowl with electric mixer until fluffy. Stir in flour mixture and orange juice until mixture is smooth. Fold in apricots and dates. Spoon batter into mold and cover with aluminum foil, securing tightly with string.
5. Place mold on a wire cake rack in pot large enough to hold mold. Pour in boiling water to a depth of 2 inches. Cover; simmer for 2 hours, replenishing water if necessary, or until a wooden skewer inserted near center comes out clean.
6. Cool in mold on wire rack 5 minutes; remove from mold. Serve warm with Orange Custard Sauce.

To reheat: Wrap in foil; heat in a preheated moderate oven (350°) for 20 minutes.

Orange Custard Sauce: Combine 1 package (3¾ ounces) vanilla flavor instant pudding and pie filling mix, ¼ cup 10X (confectioners') sugar, 2 cups milk, 1 cup orange juice and 2 tablespoons grated orange rind in a medium-size bowl; beat 1 minute with rotary beater. Beat ½ cup heavy cream until stiff; fold into orange mixture; cover; chill 1 hour. Makes about 4 cups.

Gourmet Gifts from Your Kitchen: Chili Cheese Spread, page 126; Liptauer Cheese Spread, page 126

AMARETTO BON BONS

No-bake confections of chocolate, coffee and a touch of the popular almond liqueur.

Makes about 24 one-inch balls.

1 package (6 ounces) semisweet chocolate pieces
3 tablespoons corn syrup
¼ cup superfine granulated sugar
2 teaspoons instant coffee
1 teaspoon boiling water
¼ cup almond-flavored liqueur
1 cup (approximately 24 cookies) crushed almond-flavored or shortbread cookies
½ cup chopped walnuts
Unsweetened cocoa powder

1. Combine chocolate, corn syrup, sugar, instant coffee and water in top of a double boiler. Heat over barely simmering water just until chocolate is melted; remove from heat.
2. Stir liqueur, cookie crumbs and walnuts into chocolate mixture; cool; chill.
3. Shape chocolate into 1-inch balls and roll in cocoa. Keep in tightly covered container in refrigerator.

COOKIE LETTERS

Give your favorite child a gift of a buttery, almond-filled cookie fashioned into the initial of his or her name, or give more than one to spell out NÖEL.

Bake at 375° for 10 minutes.
Makes 16 letters.

1 cup (2 sticks) butter, softened
1 cup 10X (confectioners') sugar
1 egg
1 teaspoon vanilla
2¼ cups *sifted* all-purpose flour
2 cans (8 ounces each) almond paste
⅓ cup granulated sugar
1 egg
1 teaspoon grated lemon rind
Confectioners' Icing (recipe follows)
1 tube each red and green glossy decorating gel

1. Beat butter, 10X sugar, egg and vanilla in a medium-size bowl with electric mixer until fluffy. Gradually add flour, mixing with wooden spoon until smooth and blended. Cover; chill at least 2 hours.
2. Combine almond paste, granulated sugar, remaining egg and the lemon rind in a medium-size bowl. Beat with electric mixer until smooth; chill at least 1 hour.
3. Preheat oven to 375°.
4. Roll chilled dough to a 20 × 12-inch rectangle on a lightly floured surface. Cut into 16 lengthwise strips, each 12 × 1¼-inches. Divide the almond mixture into 16 equal pieces. Roll each

piece with palms of hands into ropes 11½-inches long.
5. Place a rope of filling on each dough strip. Pinch dough around filling to enclose neatly. Shape into desired letter. Place letters about 1 inch apart on ungreased cookie sheets.
6. Bake in a preheated moderate oven (375°) for 10 minutes or until lightly browned. Cool on wire rack. Spoon Confectioners' Icing over letters to coat evenly; let dry. Decorate with red and green decorating gels.

Confectioners' Icing: Stir 2 to 3 tablespoons milk or water into 2 cups *sifted* 10X (confectioners') sugar in a small bowl to make a mixture of good spreading consistency.

CHILI CHEESE SPREAD

This zesty gift has a fiery Tex-Mex flavor. Good with taco chips.

Makes about 3 cups.

1 can (15 ounces) chili con carne with beans
1 package (8 ounces) cream cheese, softened
8 ounces sharp Cheddar cheese, shredded (2 cups)
1 tablespoon chili powder
½ cup chopped fresh parsley

Combine chili con carne, cream cheese, shredded Cheddar cheese and chili powder in a large bowl. Blend well. Turn into crock; chill until firm, at least 6 hours or overnight. Garnish with chopped parsley.

LIPTAUER CHEESE SPREAD

Piquant and mellow, this little gift is all ready to serve for a jolly gathering.

Makes about 2½ cups.

1 container (8 ounces) creamed cottage cheese
1 cup (2 sticks) butter or margarine, softened
1 tablespoon caraway seeds
1 tablespoon drained and chopped capers
1 tablespoon minced chives
1 tablespoon dry mustard
1 tablespoon drained and chopped anchovy fillets
1 tablespoon paprika
1 bunch radishes, cleaned and chopped

1. Combine cottage cheese and butter in medium-size bowl. Add caraway seeds, capers, chives, mustard, anchovies and paprika; blend well.
2. Turn into crock; chill until firm, at least 6 hours or overnight. Garnish with radishes.

BRANDIED GOLDEN FRUITCAKES

Bake loaves at 300° for 55 minutes; bake miniatures at 300° for 30 minutes.

Makes 6 small loaves or 4 dozen miniature cakes.

1 container (4 ounces) candied red cherries, halved
1 container (4 ounces) candied citron
1 cup golden raisins
1 package (8 ounces) pitted dates, chopped
½ cup brandy
3 cups *sifted* all-purpose flour
2 teaspoons baking powder
1 teaspoon ground allspice
½ teaspoon salt
1 cup (2 sticks) butter, softened
1½ cups firmly packed dark brown sugar
3 tablespoons molasses
1 teaspoon grated orange rind
6 eggs
1 cup coarsely chopped pecans
Brandy Glaze (recipe follows)
Candied cherry halves and pecans (for garnish)

1. Combine cherries, citron, raisins, dates and brandy in a medium-size bowl. Let macerate about 30 minutes.
2. Grease six 5¹¹⁄₁₆ × 3¼ × 2-inch aluminum foil pans; dust with flour; tap out excess. Or, for miniature cakes, arrange 48 (1 package) two-inch midget aluminum foil baking cups on cookie sheets.
3. Preheat oven to 300°. Sift flour, baking powder, allspice and salt onto wax paper.
4. Beat butter and sugar in a large bowl with electric mixer at medium speed until well blended. Beat in molasses and orange rind. Beat in eggs, 1 at a time, until batter is light and fluffy.
5. Stir in flour mixture gradually until smooth. Stir in fruit mixture and pecans. Divide batter equally among loaf pans or spoon batter into foil baking cups, filling ⅔ full.
6. Bake cakes in a preheated slow oven (300°), 55 minutes for loaves, 30 minutes for miniatures, or until centers spring back when lightly pressed with fingertip. Cool loaves on wire racks for 10 minutes; remove from pans; cool completely. For miniatures, cool completely in foil cups on wire racks.
7. Spoon Brandy Glaze over tops of cakes; decorate with cherry halves and pecans.

Brandy Glaze: Combine 2 cups *sifted* 10X (confectioners') sugar, 2 tablespoons orange juice and 2 teaspoons brandy in a small bowl; blend well. Makes about ½ cup.

Recipe Index

Recipe Index